Secrets

To Enliven Learning

How To Develop Extraordinary Self-Directed Training Materials

Ann Petit

Pfeiffer
& COMPANY

Amsterdam • Johannesburg • Oxford
San Diego • Sydney • Toronto

Copyright © 1994 by Ann Petit

ISBN 0-88390-416-0

Library of Congress Catalog Card Number 94-065592

Printed in the United States of America

All rights reserved

Pfeiffer & Company
International Publishers
8517 Production Avenue
San Diego, California 92121-2280
USA
(619) 578-5900; FAX (619) 578-2042

◆◆◆

To Patti Duke Kilbourne, who said I could.

◆◆◆

Contents

Overview

Welcome to *Secrets To Enliven Learning: How To Develop Extraordinary Self-Directed Training Materials*! If you're looking for a simple and effective guide to creating self-study manuals, you've come to the right place.

Whether you're a seasoned developer of self-study manuals looking for new ideas or a rookie on a first assignment, this text is for you. You'll find *Secrets To Enliven Learning* short on theory but long on practical, applicable, simple, and playful ways to create manuals.

Ordinary learning methods favor memorization and rote responses to questions; *Secrets To Enliven Learning* couples sound training practices with creativity for extraordinary results. By using the principles and methods suggested in this book, you'll set your creativity and imagination free to build self-study manuals that stand out from the rest as extraordinary in their design and effectiveness.

You'll find that being *extraordinary* rather than *ordinary* is easier than you think!

What's This Book Like?

Secrets To Enliven Learning is:

◆ Practical, emphasizing "how to" instead of "why."

◆ Fun, bringing a playful tone to the serious business of training.

◆ Digestible and temptingly served in bite-sized pieces.

◆ Simple. There's no electronic equipment to operate; turning the pages is the most complicated maneuver required.

◆ Portable. Take it anywhere, anytime; you can learn at a desk, in your favorite armchair, or on a blanket at the beach.

◆ Fast. You'll be able to complete the entire text in four to seven hours.

What's Inside?

Secrets To Enliven Learning gives you everything you'll need to successfully create self-study manuals. This book is organized into three sections and ten modules, with each module covering one of the components of extraordinary self-study manuals:

Section I, Preparation. The first section describes how to prepare the learner to learn. The four modules in this section are:

- ◆ Module 1—First Impression: Making Sure the Cover Beckons.

- ◆ Module 2—Atmospheric Conditions: Fostering a Positive Learning Environment.

- ◆ Module 3—An Ovation for Motivation: Offering Incentives To Learn.

- ◆ Module 4—Show the Way: Guiding with Clear Instructions.

Section II, Presentation. This section describes how to present the contents of your manual to the learner. The four modules included are:

- ◆ Module 5—Looking Good: Using Appearance To Aid Comprehension.

- ◆ Module 6—Watch Your Language: Using Friendly, Energetic, Understandable Words.

- ◆ Module 7—Set the Sequence: Arranging Content for Optimal Learning.

- ◆ Module 8—Word Plays: Using Words Creatively To Reinforce, Emphasize, Enliven Learning.

Section III, Practice. The final section shows you how to top off a manual with practice methods that check the learner's understanding in a nonthreatening, playful way. The two modules in this section are:

- ◆ Module 9—Topple Test Tension: Dispelling Anxiety To Promote Learning.

- ◆ Module 10—Variety Pack: Offering Practice Activities.

Instructional Design

As you use *Secrets To Enliven Learning* and begin to develop self-study manuals, you'll be working in an area known as *instructional design*, which encompasses many theories and concepts. Instructional design is a generally accepted, systematic approach to the development of instructional materials, including books such as this one. It is an orderly process, usually including three phases:

◆ An *analysis phase*, during which training needs, goals, and other factors affecting training are evaluated. This book doesn't deal with analysis.

◆ A *development phase*, during which decisions are made about content, the delivery system (such as videotape, classroom activities, and audiotape), and the creation of a manual. This book doesn't deal with the entire development phase. However, you *will* learn the most critical aspect of development, how to create self-study manuals and activities for practice.

◆ A *field-test phase*, during which the self-study manual is tested in a pilot program, assessed, and changed as necessary. This book doesn't deal with field testing.

Secrets To Enliven Learning assumes that you have concluded your analysis, defined the content of the training, and wisely selected a self-study manual as your delivery system. If you're looking for more than a handbook on the creation of self-study manuals, you need to look elsewhere. Start with the Bibliography at the end of this book, which lists resources about developing manuals as well as other aspects of instructional design.

Pondering the Future

Picture yourself a week or so into the future, just after you've completed *Secrets To Enliven Learning*. You're bursting with the knowledge you need to put together the training that your company so badly needs. You're seated at your desk, creating your development plan. You're relaxed and confident, quietly probing the corners of your imagination.

Fast-forward to eight months later. Your training program has been in use for four months, and your customers are clamoring for more self-study manuals. Your manager concludes that you're ready for greater challenges and recommends that you enroll in a five-day course in advanced training methods that you've been wanting to take.

Sound unlikely? Not if you believe it—and if you begin now to make it happen.

How To Proceed

The sequence of the sections in *Secrets To Enliven Learning* follows the usual order of training-manual development—first learner preparation, then content presentation, and finally practice. Tackle the sections in the prescribed order. The modules within each section are presented in the recommended learning sequence, but you're free to approach them in your own way. Each module stands alone; if you don't need to read a particular one, skip it.

Questions are embedded in this book, as are brief activities and "self-checks" that conclude each module. Participate actively by answering the questions and writing responses to the items in the self-checks. Following each self-check is a list of possible or suggested responses, not "correct" answers. Labeling responses as "correct" fosters correct (ordinary) thinking—the notion that only one way is "right"—whereas *Secrets To Enliven Learning* encourages extraordinary thinking. Therefore, if you come up with creative responses that do not appear in this book but certainly are relevant, congratulate yourself.

Listed in each module is the approximate time required to complete that module. If time is limited, choose a module that you can complete in the time you have.

Keep an open mind

As you go through this book, keep an open mind. Don't worry about making mistakes. Boldly take steps toward being extraordinary. If you make mistakes, consider them ordinary events on the road to extraordinary results.

Quote To Note

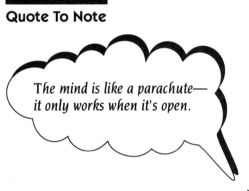

The mind is like a parachute— it only works when it's open.

Anonymous

Take charge

You're in charge from this point on. You're responsible for your own learning; there is no panel of judges to grade you. You'll profit most by investing wisely and energetically in the learning process.

Before going on, find a quiet place in which to learn. Be sure that you have sufficient light, proper ventilation, and a comfortable room temperature. Play a radio softly if it relaxes you without distracting others (or yourself). If the weather allows, go outside for a while. Your physical well-being contributes to learning, so seek a spot that lets you work in as much comfort as possible.

The only equipment you'll need is *Secrets To Enliven Learning*, a pen or a pencil, and an open mind.

Enjoy!

Section I:

Preparation

Module 1

First Impression: Making Sure the Cover Beckons

Objectives; Time and Materials Required

When you've completed this module, you'll be able to do the following:

- List three characteristics or elements to consider when creating a cover.

- State why suggesting that the learner "personalize" training materials is a good idea.

- Write two possible titles for your self-study manual.

Completing this module takes fifteen to thirty minutes. You'll need a pen or a pencil.

Where You Are in the Process

Section I: Preparation

- **First Impression: Making Sure the Cover Beckons**

- Atmospheric Conditions: Fostering a Positive Learning Environment

- An Ovation for Motivation: Offering Incentives To Learn

- Show the Way: Guiding with Clear Instructions

Section II: Presentation

- Looking Good: Using Appearance To Aid Comprehension

- Watch Your Language: Using Friendly, Energetic, Understandable Words

- Set the Sequence: Arranging Content for Optimal Learning

- Word Plays: Using Words Creatively To Reinforce, Emphasize, Enliven Learning

Section III: Practice

- Topple Test Tension: Dispelling Anxiety To Promote Learning

- Variety Pack: Offering Practice Activities

Preview

The learner's first impression of a self-study manual immediately colors his or her emotional and intellectual response to learning. That first impression can be made positive by painting the learning experience in warm, bright colors instead of a chilling, deadly black.

Many learners know what it's like to be presented with a three-inch black binder spilling over with pages. "Here's your manual," says the trainer. "Everything you need is in here." This experience can be so formidable that the learner's interest evaporates.

But the introduction to training doesn't have to be that way. You can make the learner want to know what's in your manual by packaging it in a cover that invites rather than repels. You can either settle for the ordinary or target the *extraordinary*.

Think about your own experiences with covers. When scanning magazine racks for some leisure reading, what catches your eye? Circle the features that you find more appealing:

DULL COLORS	or	BRIGHT COLORS
CRAMMED SPACE	or	OPEN SPACE
MAULED COVERS	or	PRISTINE COVERS
SMUDGED COPY	or	SPOTLESS COPY
SOMBER TONE	or	CHEERFUL TONE

Most people will be lured into buying a magazine by the characteristics on the right. Go beyond the ordinary by packaging your manuals in a way that will compel the learner to "buy" them.

Well begun is half done.

Anonymous

Here's How

Here's how to create a cover that beckons:

1. ***Illustrate the cover.*** Consider computer graphics, professional illustrations, or simple sketches. Illustrations don't have to bankrupt your training budget; be creative and seek alternatives to the ordinary. Learn to draw. A self-study text called *Fundamentals of Graphic Images*, which is listed in the Bibliography, can help.

Figure 1 offers an example of an effectively illustrated cover.

Figure 1. An Effectively Illustrated Cover

2. **Color the cover.** Put plenty of color on the cover, using no more than three or four different colors. If a tight budget restricts you to one or two, use different screen tints to give the impression of more color.

If you can use as many as four colors, you will be able to create an unlimited number of colors by using four-color process colors for your printing. The printer who will be printing your cover is the best source of help and information.

Figure 2 presents an example of the effective use of color (designated by different percentages of screen tints).

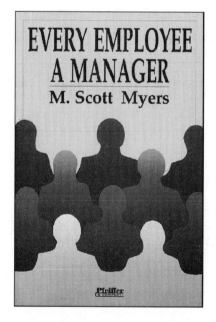

Figure 2. The Effective Use of Color (Screen Tints) on a Cover

3. **Use white space.** White space, which is simply open space without type or figures, avoids a chaotic look and highlights what you want the learner to notice on the cover. White space can make a cover more inviting and dramatic. The contents of the book, your judgment, your style, and the message you want to convey to a learner are all factors in deciding how much white space to use. There is no rule governing how much "white is right" on a cover.

One way to consider the effects of white space is to look at other books. The next time you're in a bookstore, pay attention to which book covers catch your eye. The chances are that many of the compelling ones consist mainly of white space. When in doubt, err on the side of more white space.

In Figures 1 and 2, note how the white space dramatizes the title.

4. **Play the name game; title creatively.** Give your self-study manual a title that intrigues, one with some zip and imagination. The title should succinctly capture the training topic and should make the benefits of the training apparent to the learner.

For example, a manual about telephone-service training could be entitled *On Call: 10 Easy Steps to Superior Service* instead of simply *Telephone-Service Training*. Similarly, a manual on telephone sales could be entitled *Dialing for Dollars* instead of simply *Telephone-Sales Training*.

5. **Splurge on bindings.** Explore different types of bindings. Choose one that's suitable for the purpose and size of your manual, even if it costs a bit more than you'd hoped to spend. Some of your choices are shown in Table 1. Then refer to Table 2 for factors to take into consideration when assessing alternatives for binding your self-study manual.

Consult professionals for alternatives and cost estimates, but always keep your learners in mind when you make your choice.

Table 1. Types of Bindings

Binding Type	Description
GBC Comb	A continuous plastic strip with interlocking teeth is run through holes at the edge of the pages.
Saddle Stitch	Sheets of paper that are 8½" x 22", for example, are folded in half to create 8½" x 11" pages. Staples are placed in the center of the sheets along the fold.
Spiral Binding	A continuously spiraling length of metal or plastic is run through holes at the edge of the pages.
Thermal Binding	Page edges are aligned between the front and back covers. A glued strip of material is run down the side or "spine," attaching all pages and both covers to one another.
Perfect Binding	The front cover, the back cover, and the spine are produced in one piece. As the pages come off the press, they are dipped in hot glue and centered on the spine. Then the whole book is cut to size, and the front cover and the back cover are pressed into place.
Wire "O"	This binding is a combination of a GBC comb and a spiral binding. Small, linked spirals replace the square "teeth" of the GBC comb.
Three-Ring Binder	This enduring classic is available in almost any color or size and can have a hard or soft cover.

Table 2. Factors To Consider in Selecting Bindings

Factor	Related Issues
Number of pages	Some types of binding restrict the number of pages you can include.
Durability	How long is the manual expected to last? Will it be tossed around and abused or treated with kindness?
Revisions and additions	Will you need to periodically replace or add pages to the text, or will the entire contents endure for years?
Cost	The more complicated the binding process, the more you'll pay per unit. (For example, ringed binders are simple and inexpensive, whereas saddle stitching is more complicated and costlier.)
Volume	Plan ahead to save money. Depending on your binding selection, you'll incur at least a minimum setup charge. So order enough units to avoid a charge that exceeds the minimum. You may also see a per-unit discount for ordering in quantity.
Expected Use	How will the learner use the manual? Does it have to stand up, lay flat, be held in the hands, or be used in a limited amount of space?
Page Size	Standard page size is 8½" x 11". If you want smaller pages, such as 8" x 10", be aware that custom-sized pages usually cost more and the binding probably will, too.

6. **Don't bulk up.** Refrain from using bulky binders. They're unwieldy and intimidating. Anything over two inches is probably too large. Use several smaller binders instead.

7. **Allow for expansion.** Allow extra space for possible revisions and additions or for the learner to insert pages of his or her own. Avoid stuffing binders.

8. **Provide new manuals.** Supply each learner with a new self-study manual. Encourage learners to personalize their manuals with their own materials or artwork. The process of personalizing makes learners comfortable with the new text and fosters ownership of the learning as well as the material to be learned.

9. **Use tabs.** Break up large sections of your manual with tabs that name, not just number, each section. For example, a tab should say "Introduction" rather than "Section 1." If the learner will be flipping back and forth between sections, consider labeling both sides of the tab.

Exercise Your Mind

In your experience as a learner, what has created a positive first impression for you? Write your recollections here, and remember your experience when creating a first impression.

_____

_____

_____

_____

_____

_____

_____

_____

_____

_____

_____

_____

Highlights of This Module

First impressions are lasting. The cover of your manual should draw the learner into learning, not away from it. Consider features such as illustrations, color, white space, and an engaging title. Choose a binding that works for the learner; consider size, durability, revisions and additions, and expected use. Then see a professional for alternatives. Encourage personalization, and label sections for ease of use. Strive to make an *extraordinary* first impression.

Self-Check for Module 1

Take a few moments now to check your understanding of what you've read. Feel free to look up answers in this module.

1. Name three characteristics or elements to consider when creating a positive first impression.

_____

_____

_____

_____

2. Explain why it's a good idea to allow the learner to personalize training materials.

_____

_____

_____

_____

3. Write at least two possible titles for your self-study manual. Each title should state the topic and the benefits of the manual and should pique the learner's interest. Use subtitles if you wish.

_____

_____

_____

_____

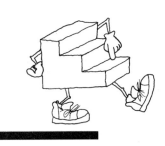

Your Next Step

Compare your work with the responses on page 26.

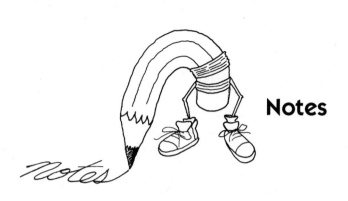

Notes

Responses to Self-Check for Module 1

Suggested responses are as follows. Any responses you wrote are fine as long as they capture the basic content noted here. And if you came up with something especially creative, that's great.

1. Name three characteristics or elements to consider when creating a positive first impression.

   Illustrations
   Color
   White space
   Engaging title

2. Explain why it's a good idea to allow the learner to personalize training materials.

   Personalizing training materials may instill a sense of ownership of the training and the materials themselves, and it makes the learner feel comfortable with the text.

3. Write at least two possible titles for your self-study manual. Each title should state the topic and the benefits of the manual and should pique the learner's interest. Use subtitles if you wish.

   Virtually any answer that contributes to a good first impression is a correct one. So congratulate yourself for your efforts, and give yourself special kudos for imaginative titles.

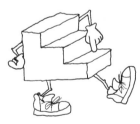

Your Next Step

Continue working through the book or take a break. It's your choice.

Module 2

Atmospheric Conditions: Fostering a Positive Learning Environment

Objectives; Time and Materials Required

When you've completed this module, you'll be able to do the following:

◆ Describe three ways to get the learner's attention.

◆ Name two methods for overcoming the learner's fear of failure.

◆ List the physical and environmental conditions that affect learning.

Completing this module takes fifteen to thirty minutes. You'll need a pen or a pencil.

Where You Are in the Process

Section I: Preparation

- ◆ First Impression: Making Sure the Cover Beckons

- ◆ **Atmospheric Conditions: Fostering a Positive Learning Environment**

- ◆ An Ovation for Motivation: Offering Incentives To Learn

- ◆ Show the Way: Guiding with clear instructions

Section II: Presentation

- ◆ Looking Good: Using Appearance To Aid Comprehension

- ◆ Watch Your Language: Using Friendly, Energetic, Understandable Words

- ◆ Set the Sequence: Arranging Content for Optimal Learning

- ◆ Word Plays: Using Words Creatively To Reinforce, Emphasize, Enliven Learning

Section III: Practice

- ◆ Topple Test Tension: Dispelling Anxiety To Promote Learning

- ◆ Variety Pack: Offering Practice Activities

Preview

Have you ever been anxious about learning or felt that the material was hard to understand or just boring? Do you recall any training that took place in a stifling and/or uncomfortable place? Many learners have had such experiences.

Ideal atmospheric conditions are emotionally, intellectually, and physically comfortable for the learner. A comfortable and friendly environment is conducive to learning; an intimidating environment is not.

To construct ideal atmospheric conditions, you need to do four things: (1) get the learner's attention, (2) allay the learner's fear of failure, (3) foster a relaxed frame of mind, and (4) encourage learning.

Here's How

Here's how to foster a positive learning environment:

1. **_Get the learner's attention._** Your first goal is to make the learner interested in what lies ahead by using an attention-getting technique. Consider your own experience with self-study manuals. What gets your attention? A lengthy, dull preface or a short, lively one? A jam-packed, intimidating table of contents or a crisp, interest-piquing one? Search your imagination for an interest builder that leaves ordinary starts at the starting line.

To stimulate learner interest, try one of these approaches:

◆ *Offer an anecdote related to your training topic.* For example, if the manual trains the learner to interview potential job candidates, tell the learner about the most inept interview you've conducted and how the techniques in the manual would have helped.

◆ *Use a cartoon or other gentle humor related to the topic.* Read comics, magazines, and other materials for potential items to include in your self-study manuals. Draw your own cartoons if the spirit moves you; even an amateurish cartoon can be an effective communication tool.

♦ *Ask a thought-provoking question.* For example, in a manual on customer-service training, you might ask, "How often has a customer been frustrated and angry on the phone, and how often have you wished you knew how to turn the situation around?" Stimulate interest in learning with questions that your manual will help answer.

Rhyme Time

To get attention,
you could mention
A tale, a cartoon,
or a question.

♦ *Illustrate the training topic.* For example, in a module on human anatomy you might provide a drawing of a skeleton with bones labeled in layman's terms, such as "funny bone" and "breastbone." Explain that the learner is mastering a new language and soon will be able to relabel the skeleton in medical terminology, substituting "humerus" and "sternum" for "funny bone" and "breastbone," respectively.

♦ *Quote a startling statistic that will interest and surprise the learner.* For example, you might say, "The average corporate training budget has been slashed by 20 percent since 1987. This means that you must find faster and less costly ways to train without sacrificing quality."

◆ *Begin with a welcoming statement from the company's chief executive officer.* The statement can be written, audiotaped, or videotaped and then duplicated in your self-study manual. Compare these two examples of a welcoming statement:

Example 1: This training program is for the customer-service representative (CSR). The CSR is very important to Bioteam, Inc., because Bioteam's customers are important. Our customers are demanding and expect that the CSRs will answer all their questions about rigidifiers, stiltometers, ASGs, and other flexillators. The training program is not easy and the dropout rate is high, but the rewards of the CSR's job are worth it. Good luck.

Example 2: Welcome to *On the Front Line: Armed with Superior Service Skills.* This training program is designed to equip you, the customer-service associate, with the skills you'll need to excel in your new job. When you have completed the program, you'll join hundreds of other successful graduates who form the front line of our premiere customer-service organization. I'm pleased that you decided to join an organization renowned for its quality and service, an organization of which I am very proud.

Sincerely,

Theresa Benedetto
Vice President, Customer Service
Bioteam, Inc.

Which statement, Example 1 or Example 2, will get the learner's attention and serve as a welcome? Why? Write your response in the following space.

_____

_____

_____

_____

Example 2 is the better statement. Ms. Benedetto expresses her confidence in the learner's ability to excel, noting that many others have been successful. Her welcome is warm, personal, simple, and straightforward.

The unidentified author of the first statement uses jargon, says that many learners aren't successful, and employs an impersonal tone. The author grabs the learner's attention—but fails to welcome the learner and instead produces a great deal of anxiety.

2. **Allay the learner's fear of failure.** Your second goal is to put the learner at ease by allaying fear of failure. Some learners are overwhelmed with anxiety about learning; others may recall and focus on negative learning experiences from the past. Some learners may have been out of school for a long time and worry about their performance. Generally, you can expect most learners to have some degree of fear about learning. Here are some tips for reducing a learner's fear of failure:

- *Express great confidence in the learner's ability to succeed.* Include a statement like this one: "This is all new to you, so you can expect to feel a little anxiety about it. Put that aside as much as you can. You're here because someone had confidence in your eventual success. Show that someone that he or she was right."

- *Tell the learner that making mistakes is a normal and natural part of learning.* Everyone stumbles now and then.

- *Advise the learner that the training is "open book."* Instant memorization is not expected; information can always be looked up.

- *Remind the learner that this training is a self-paced program controlled by the learner, not a race.* Comprehension and subsequent application are the goals, not speed.

◆ *Let the learner know that the manual can serve as an on-the-job reference later.* You might even want to include the following quote:

Quote To Note

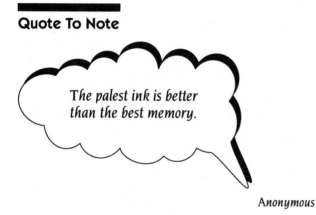

The palest ink is better than the best memory.

Anonymous

◆ *Offer the learner an endorsement from someone who completed training and successfully applied new learning despite an initial fear of failure.* You need a statement like this one: "I was really worried about the training program. I hadn't had formal training or taken a course in more than three years. But it was great! The whole thing was so nonthreatening that I eventually forgot what I was afraid of. All that worrying for nothing!" The endorsement can be written, audiotaped, videotaped, or stated in person.

◆ Suggest that the learner try using affirmations, which replace negative emotions (like fear) with positive ones (like confidence). An affirmation is simply a positive thought that's frequently repeated, either aloud or to oneself, such as "I'm confident that I'll excel in this program." Not all learners will buy the idea of affirmations; but some will, and the affirmations they choose may help.

Regardless of which methods you choose for helping the learner overcome fear of failure, use them early in training. Then sprinkle your self-study manual liberally with expressions of your confidence in the learner's ability to achieve success.

3. **_Foster a relaxed frame of mind._** Your third goal is to foster a relaxed (but alert) frame of mind on the part of the learner by using a friendly writing style. Here are some tips on how to create a bond with the learner:

◆ Use simple, everyday words that are familiar to the learner.

◆ Use contractions so that your writing reads like conversation.

◆ Address the learner as "you" instead of "the learner."

Start a conversation, not a lecture. (This subject is discussed in greater detail in the module entitled "Watch Your Language: Using Friendly, Energetic, Understandable Words.")

4. **Encourage learning.** Your fourth goal is to encourage learning by providing or offering advice about appropriate physical surroundings. Whether you are responsible for the learning environment or the learner is working alone, without the benefit of your personal help, the learner must have a special place to work, befitting the importance of the learning. If the learner is stuck in a shabby corner of the mail room, he or she will perceive the learning as an activity that is both unseen and unimportant. Consequently, these suggestions about environmental elements should be stated in your manual:

◆ Sit in a comfortable chair, preferably one with adjustable height and back position.

◆ Use a fair-sized desk or other working surface; check for adequate personal storage space.

◆ Be sure you have access to all of the equipment needed to work through the manual.

◆ Make sure that there is adequate lighting, preferably natural light.

◆ Find a spot with a low noise level, or do what you can to minimize noise, including asking others in the area to be considerate.

◆ Use headphones to provide a musical background if desired.

- ◆ Avoid rooms with a cluttered, distracting appearance. Colors like pale blue or green are most relaxing for the learner. However, professional environments are often beige, gray, or similar colors, and such muted tones are fine. The important thing is that the background should soothe, not shout.

- ◆ Check the room temperature; research shows that a temperature of 68 degrees Fahrenheit is comfortable for most people.

- ◆ Check for adequate ventilation without drafts.

- ◆ Personalize the learning space with pictures, knickknacks, and other items if considerable time will be spent in the area.

These suggestions lead to an ideal learning environment. Encourage the learner to come as close to the ideal as possible, concentrating primarily on finding a spot that is comfortable for him or her.

Exercise Your Mind

What other physical and environmental conditions might impede or improve learning?

_____

_____

_____

_____

_____

_____

_____

_____

Highlights of This Module

Construct atmospheric conditions that are comfortable and conducive to learning. Get the learner's attention with anecdotes, cartoons, questions, or other means. Alleviate fear of failure by saying that mistakes are normal and natural, by expressing confidence in the learner's ability, and by explaining that each learner should set his or her own pace. Use a friendly, conversational tone to foster a relaxed, alert frame of mind on the part of the learner. Consider (or encourage the learner to consider) equipment, light, noise, color, temperature, and ventilation. Bypass the ordinary in favor of the *extraordinary*.

Self-Check for Module 2

Take a few moments now to assess your understanding, looking back through Module 2 as needed.

1. List three techniques for getting the learner's attention.

_____

_____

_____

_____

2. List two ways to allay the learner's fear of failure.

_____

_____

_____

3. Name at least three atmospheric conditions to assess when considering the physical setting for learning.

_____

_____

_____

_____

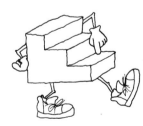

Your Next Step

Check your responses with those on page 42.

Notes

Responses to Self-Check for Module 2

The following are suggested responses:

1. List three techniques for getting the learner's attention.

   An anecdote
   A cartoon or other gentle humor
   A thought-provoking question
   An illustration
   A statistic
   A welcoming statement

2. List two ways to allay the learner's fear of failure.

   Saying that mistakes are normal and natural
   Assuring the learner that he or she is not expected to remember
     every single thing
   Reminding the learner that the manual can serve as an on-the-job
     reference later
   Inviting the learner to set his or her own pace
   Expressing confidence in the learner's ability to succeed
   Advising the learner that training is "open book"
   Offering an endorsement from a successful learner
   Suggesting affirmations

3. Name at least three atmospheric conditions to assess when
   considering the physical setting for learning.

   A comfortable chair
   A fair-sized desk with storage space
   All equipment required to work through the manual
   Adequate lighting
   A low noise level
   Headphones for music (if desired)
   An uncluttered background with soothing colors
   A comfortable room temperature
   Adequate ventilation
   A personalized learning space

Good job! Use what you've learned here and your own instincts and experience to create ideal atmospheric conditions.

Your Next Step

Take a look at Table 3 on the next page, and use this checklist when you begin to design a self-study manual. Then decide whether to tackle another module in this book or take a break.

Table 3. Atmospheric Conditions Checklist*

Have you considered these aspects of the physical learning environment?	Have you considered these aspects of the emotional and intellectual learning environment?
◆ Comfortable chair	◆ Conversational tone
◆ Desk with storage	◆ Simple, everyday language
◆ All needed equipment	◆ Mistakes are O.K.
◆ Sufficient light	◆ Express confidence in learner
◆ Low noise level	◆ Learner sets pace
◆ Musical background (if desired)	◆ Provocative questions
◆ Soothing wall colors	◆ Gentle humor
◆ Temperature	◆ Anecdote
◆ Ventilation	◆ Illustration
◆ Personalization	◆ Welcoming statement

*This table may be freely reproduced for educational/training activities. There is no requirement to obtain special permission for such uses. Please make sure that the following statement appears on all reproductions:

Module 3

An Ovation for Motivation: Offering Incentives To Learn

Objectives; Time and Materials Required

When you've completed this module, you'll be able to do the following:

- List four ways to motivate the learner.

- Identify three characteristics of a sound learning objective.

- List two ways to recognize and reward the learner.

Completing this module takes fifteen to thirty minutes. You'll need a pen or a pencil.

Where You Are in the Process

Section I: Preparation

- ◆ First Impression: Making Sure the Cover Beckons

- ◆ Atmospheric Conditions: Fostering a Positive Learning Environment

- ◆ **An Ovation for Motivation: Offering Incentives To Learn**

- ◆ Show the Way: Guiding with Clear Instructions

Section II: Presentation

- ◆ Looking Good: Using Appearance To Aid Comprehension

- ◆ Watch Your Language: Using Friendly, Energetic, Understandable Words

- ◆ Set the Sequence: Arranging Content for Optimal Learning

- ◆ Word Plays: Using Words Creatively To Reinforce, Emphasize, Enliven Learning

Section III: Practice

- ◆ Topple Test Tension: Dispelling Anxiety To Promote Learning

- ◆ Variety Pack: Offering Practice Activities

Preview

Motivation is a frequently overlooked aspect of developing self-study manuals.

But beware! Nothing you do can really motivate the learner. The best you can do is to offer incentives that may spur the learner's ambition. You provide the incentives; the learner provides the motivation. As the anonymous saying goes, "You can take the learner to training, but you can't make the learner think."

Incentives take many forms, and the ones that reach a particular learner depend on that learner. These methods have been found effective in the context of a self-study manual: (1) citing the objectives of the training, (2) stating the benefits to the learner, (3) giving the responsibility for learning to the learner, and (4) recognizing and rewarding the learner.

Remember that highly motivated learners will perform *extraordinarily* well.

Here's How

Here's how to offer incentives to learn:

1. ***Cite the objectives of the training.*** Objectives are widely acknowledged as vital ingredients in instructional design. They identify the expected outcomes of learning in specific, easy-to-understand, concrete terms, not in vague, hopeful abstractions.

Learning without objectives is highly objectionable! Learners like to know what is expected of them. Tell them by citing the learning objectives.

Consider the content and intent of your self-study manual, and answer this question: *On completion of this manual, what will the learner be able to do or know that he or she could not do or did not know before?*

Keep your answer short and simple, yet specific. Use descriptive, active verbs in your answer, such as "construct," "encode," "select," "label," "list," "identify," "define," and "draw." Be certain that the objective is important to the learner. Make sure that it is measurable; that is, include a way to measure precisely what (and sometimes how well) the learner is able to do or know.

Sound difficult? It may seem so before you've written any objectives, but after some practice it won't be. Just remember to use the simple 3S-I-M pattern:

Make It

Short

Simple

Specific

Important

Measurable

Here are a few examples of sound learning objectives:

◆ "Within fifteen seconds you'll be able to select the correct code for the procedure from a list of fifty."

◆ "You'll be able to describe four techniques for diffusing anger and the situations in which they're most appropriate."

◆ "You'll be able to cite three key functions of a team coach."

Learning objectives are a cornerstone of instructional design; they have been exhaustively researched and documented. *Secrets To Enliven Learning* contains but a speck of information about creating learning objectives. For a more detailed yet easy-to-use resource, consult Robert Mager's (1984) *Preparing Instructional Objectives* (see the Bibliography).

Exercise Your Mind

Try your hand at writing a few learning objectives for your training modules. Adhere to the 3S-I-M pattern.

_____

_____

_____

_____

_____

_____

_____

_____

_____

2. **State the benefits to the learner.** Citing the learning objectives isn't enough. Even after reading the objectives, the learner may be thinking, "So what? Why should I care? What's in it for me?" If the learner can't see the value of the training, he or she won't devote the energy and enthusiasm needed to make learning *extraordinary*.

Consider the benefits carefully—not the benefits to the company, the community, or the common good, but to the *individual learner*. Relate the benefits to performance on the job. How will the learner's work be simplified, made more efficient, less aggravating? Be enthusiastic and realistic in telling the learner what benefits he or she can expect from the learning.

Here are some examples:

◆ "A recent graduate said of this self-study manual, 'This was the best negotiation training I ever had. My contracting ratio went up 23 percent, and I received a large bonus!'"

◆ "Once you've completed this course in performance management, you'll find writing annual performance appraisals much easier. You'll take less time, feel less aggravated, and achieve greater acceptance from your employees."

◆ "Stop the endless cycle of interviewing! Get off the turnover treadmill! After this training in behavioral interviewing, you'll choose the best person for the job the first time around."

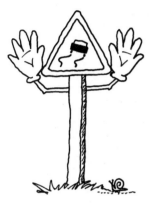

Caution!

Objectives and benefits can seem similar. Remember that objectives tell the learner what he or she will be able to do or know, whereas benefits say why the new skill or knowledge is important to the learner. Objectives are specific; benefits are general. Tell the learner about both, and you can't go wrong.

Exercise Your Mind

What benefits does your own self-study manual offer the learner?

_____

_____

_____

_____

_____

_____

_____

3. **_Give the responsibility for learning to the learner._** To make sure that the learner assumes responsibility for learning, follow these guidelines:

♦ _Let the learner establish ownership of the learning process._ Place your trust in the learner to be responsible for his or her actions and efforts. If your self-study manual is to be a self-study project, only the learner can be in charge.

♦ _Say that the learner is responsible for learning._ A simple statement such as the following is all it takes: "The responsibility for learning is in your hands now."

♦ _Suggest—don't demand—that the learner actively participate, noting why participation is important._ Say something like this: "Your full participation, through attentiveness and completion of activities, will help you get the most from this manual."

♦ _Give as many choices as possible to increase the amount of control that the learner has._ Here are some examples:

▲ Whenever possible, allow the learner to decide the sequence of learning. Construct independent modules that let the learner step out of your prescribed order.

▲ Supplement the written material with audiotape and videotape. Allow the learner to use the medium of his or her choice.

▲ Consider giving the learner a deed to learning that is a tangible form of learning ownership.

4. **_Recognize and reward the learner._** In a self-study setting you won't really know what the learner is doing. So expect the best, and the learner will rise to your expectations. Acknowledge the learner's efforts by recognizing and rewarding him or her.

Sprinkle your text liberally with declarations of recognition:

- ◆ "How did you do on the exercise? That's great! Even if you didn't get all the answers, you can always go back and look them up."

- ◆ "Pat yourself on the back for completing this exercise. It was an especially difficult one."

Discuss the possibility of more tangible rewards with your manager. Here are some examples of inexpensive rewards to offer the learner:

- ◆ "When you've successfully completed Sections A through E, you'll receive a $25 gift certificate for the store of your choice."

- ◆ "At the completion of each module, you'll receive a certificate worth two hours off with pay."

- ◆ "When you've completed the program, you'll be given a brass desk clock with your name engraved on it."

Tangible rewards are strong motivators.

Highlights of This Module

Offer the learner incentives designed to motivate him or her in the direction of learning. Construct short, simple, specific, important, and measurable objectives. Describe the benefits of learning, and grant ownership of the learning to the learner. Frequently recognize the learner's efforts, and offer tangible rewards if possible. Lead the learner toward the achievement of *extraordinary* results.

Self-Check for Module 3

Pause a moment to measure your understanding of the ideas presented in this module. Look back in the text if you like, and look within yourself for creative answers as well.

1. List four ways to offer incentives that may motivate the learner.

_____

_____

_____

_____

2. Identify at least three characteristics of a good learning objective.

_____

_____

_____

3. Name two ways to recognize and reward the learner.

_____

_____

Your Next Step

Check your responses with those on page 56.

Responses to Self-Check for Module 3

The author suggests these responses:

1. List four ways to offer incentives that may motivate the learner.

   Cite learning objectives.
   State benefits to the learner.
   Make the learner responsible for learning.
   Offer recognition and rewards.

2. Identify at least three characteristics of a good learning objective.

   Short
   Simple
   Specific
   Important
   Measurable

3. Name two ways to recognize and reward the learner.

   Make declarations of recognition.
   Offer tangible rewards whenever possible.

   How did you do? If you've done your best, congratulations for trying! And if you've come up with additional creative answers of your own, give yourself an extra pat on the back.

Your Next Step

Consider starting another module or take a break.

Module 4

Show the Way: Guiding with Clear Instructions

Objectives; Time and Materials Required

When you've completed this module, you'll be able to do the following:

- List four items of information that show the learner the way to proceed through your self-study manual.

- Name three types of instruction to give the learner.

- Explain the purpose of a course map.

Completing this module requires thirty to forty-five minutes. You'll need a pen or a pencil.

Where You Are in the Process

Section I: Preparation

♦ First Impression: Making Sure the Cover Beckons

♦ Atmospheric Conditions: Fostering a Positive Learning Environment

♦ An Ovation for Motivation: Offering Incentives To Learn

♦ **Show the Way: Guiding with Clear Instructions**

You Are Here

Section II: Presentation

♦ Looking Good: Using Appearance To Aid Comprehension

♦ Watch Your Language: Using Friendly, Energetic, Understandable Words

♦ Set the Sequence: Arranging Content for Optimal Learning

♦ Word Plays: Using Words Creatively To Reinforce, Emphasize, Enliven Learning

Section III: Practice

♦ Topple Test Tension: Dispelling Anxiety To Promote Learning

♦ Variety Pack: Offering Practice Activities

Preview

When you need to travel to a new place, you need information. You need confirmation that you've selected the proper destination and that you have what's needed to make the most of the journey; you need directions and you need an itinerary. Whether you're on a new hiking trail or you're trying to find Space Mountain at Disneyland, you need information that shows you the way.

A learner in unfamiliar territory, traveling on the path to successful learning, needs similar information. There are four items of information that you should give a learner: (1) the big picture, (2) prerequisites, (3) instructions for use, and (4) a course map.

By providing these four items of information, you'll show the learner the way through a new land—your manual.

Here's How

Here's how to guide the learner through the manual:

1. ***Give the big picture.*** The big picture tells where the learner is headed, enabling him or her to decide whether the right destination has been chosen. Imagine finding yourself on the wrong bus, heading for Boca Raton instead of Baton Rouge! The purpose of identifying the destination in broad, general terms is to help the learner avoid a long journey on the wrong bus.

To give the big picture, write a short sentence that lets the learner know that he or she is on the right bus. Here are some examples:

- ◆ "This self-study manual shows you how to delegate with confidence."

- ◆ "You'll learn how to develop a self-study manual of your own."

- ◆ "This text prepares you to design financial reports for the layperson."

Exercise Your Mind

Stop a moment and write a sentence or two about the big picture for your own self-study manual.

_____

_____

_____

_____

_____

_____

2. **Identify prerequisites.** Prerequisites state the skills and knowledge that the learner must have *before* tackling your self-study manual. The purpose of identifying prerequisites is to make sure that the learner is prepared for what lies ahead; prerequisites prevent the learner from boarding the bus without what's needed to obtain the greatest value from the journey.

For each manual you create, answer this question: "What must the learner know or be able to do before beginning the journey?" Answer the question with a short statement. Here are some examples:

- "Before beginning this manual, you should know how to conjugate a verb."

- "This text assumes that you have interviewed at least twenty job candidates."

- "This manual assumes that you know how to read a topographical map."

Defining prerequisites is essential for *extraordinary* learning.

3. **Provide instructions for use.** Just as a traveler needs directions to a destination, the learner needs to know how to use your self-study manual. What may seem obvious to you because you are intimately acquainted with your manual may be obscure to the learner. Here are some types of instructions that you might consider:

◆ *Briefly describe how the manual is organized.* For example, you might say, "The text is organized into four sections, each containing five modules."

◆ *Explain the sequence of learning.* Perhaps the learner must follow a prescribed order, perhaps not. Maybe the learner only needs part of what you've developed. Tell the learner what the choices are. For example, you might say, "You may select the order in which you want to study the sections, but you must complete a section's modules in the order in which they appear."

◆ *Talk about self-evaluations and practice.* What should the learner expect? (Are the answers given? Is there a scoring sheet? Is there a separate workbook?) You might say, "Each module is followed by a short quiz that enables you to check your understanding."

◆ *Explain that the manual belongs to the learner.* He or she may write in it, insert pages, or draw mustaches on faces if desired.

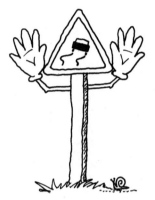

Caution!

If you have a lot of difficulty writing instructions or you end up with four pages' worth, your manual is probably too complicated to use. In this case consider simplifying the manual.

Exercise Your Mind

What are some instructions that you plan on giving the user of your self-study manual?

_____

_____

_____

_____

_____

_____

_____

_____

4. **Draw a course map.** A course map serves as an itinerary for the learner's journey through your self-study manual. The purpose of a course map is to show what to expect along the way, where to stop, where the learner is at any particular point, when to take breaks, and when the journey ends.

A course map can be a straightforward depiction of the learner's itinerary (as the one in this book is), or it can be an inventive illustration of the journey. To create your own course map, follow these steps:

- ◆ Determine the starting point.

- ◆ List all modules in the training program.

- ◆ Calculate approximate "travel times" for each module.

- ◆ Identify points where important activities take place, such as reviews, practice on real forms, and breaks in the action.

- ◆ Plot a route through the program, considering alternate routes or shortcuts that the learner can take.

After you've completed these steps, put all the elements together imaginatively in a course map. Think of a course map as just that—a map—and try your hand at sketching it. Here are two ideas for sketching course maps:

- ◆ Use a race course as a model, with obstacles, a starting line, and a finishing line.

- ◆ Use a road map as a model, with sharp turns, hills, and stops along the way.

If you were developing a manual for city planners, for example, you might want a course map based on a road map for a city. In that case you would include items such as the following:

- Streets and street signs.

- Bodies of water and bridges to cross them.

- Compass headings in the margins of the map.

- Golf courses and other recreational areas.

- Landmarks that represent course modules.

Finally, you might fold the course map like a street map and insert it in your self-study manual.

Play with ideas for course maps. Think about the different kinds of maps you've seen or used: road maps, trail maps, treasure-hunt maps, maps to movie stars' homes, navigational maps, and so on. Think about the information on them and how these maps are used. Then set your imagination free. Haven't you sketched directions for someone at some time? That's all a course map is—a place to start, a route to follow, details of what will happen along the way, and a destination.

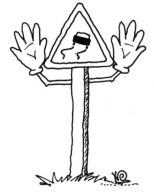

Caution!

A great course map isn't a substitute for a table of contents. Once the learner has completed the training modules, referring to the table of contents is the easiest, quickest way to find information. Use the table of contents in this book as a model for devising your own.

Highlights of This Module

Show the way through your manual by giving the learner needed information: (1) The big picture, so that the learner can determine whether the proper destination has been selected; (2) prerequisites, so that the learner understands what to have or know how to do before starting the journey; (3) instructions for using the manual; and (4) a course map that lays out the journey in detail. Send the learner off in an *extraordinary* way.

Self-Check for Module 4

Take a few minutes now to check your understanding of how to show the learner the way. Feel free to look back in the module for answers.

1. List the four items of information that the learner needs in order to be prepared for the journey through a self-study manual.

_____

_____

_____

_____

2. Name three topics that should be covered when giving the learner instructions for using a manual.

_____

_____

_____

3. Explain the purpose of a course map.

_____

_____

_____

Your Next Step

Compare what you've written with the responses on page 68.

Responses to Self-Check for Module 4

The following are suggested responses. If you've come up with additional creative responses, so much the better!

1. List the four items of information that the learner needs in order to be prepared for the journey through a self-study manual.

   The big picture
   Prerequisites
   Instructions for use
   A course map

2. Name three topics that should be covered when giving the learner instructions for using a manual.

   The organization of the manual
   The sequence of learning
   Self-evaluations and practice
   The learner's ownership of the manual

3. Explain the purpose of a course map.

   To show the learner what to expect along the way, where to stop, where the learner is at any particular point, and when the journey ends

   How did you do? Congratulations on an energetic effort!

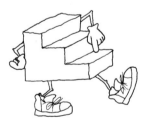

Your Next Step

If you've completed the modules in Section I: Preparation in the order of presentation, you've come to the end of the line. Treat yourself to a small token of achievement—a candy bar, a phone call to a friend, or a Ferrari. Your choice!

Your next steps will be to embark on Section II: Presentation and then Section III: Practice.

Section II:

Presentation

Module 5

Looking Good: Using Appearance To Aid Comprehension

Objectives; Time and Materials Required

When you've completed this module, you'll be able to do the following:

◆ Identify the best way to locate information in a manual.

◆ State the maximum number of type styles that should be used in a manual.

◆ List three ways to present information with a minimum number of words.

Completing this module requires forty-five minutes to an hour. You'll need a pen or a pencil.

Where You Are in the Process

Section I: Preparation

- ◆ First Impression: Making Sure the Cover Beckons

- ◆ Atmospheric Conditions: Fostering a Positive Learning Environment

- ◆ An Ovation for Motivation: Offering Incentives To Learn

- ◆ Show the Way: Guiding with Clear Instructions

Section II: Presentation

- ◆ **Looking Good: Using Appearance To Aid Comprehension**

- ◆ Watch Your Language: Using Friendly, Energetic, Understandable Words

- ◆ Set the Sequence: Arranging Content for Optimal Learning

- ◆ Word Plays: Using Words Creatively To Reinforce, Emphasize, Enliven Learning

Section III: Practice

- ◆ Topple Test Tension: Dispelling Anxiety To Promote Learning

- ◆ Variety Pack: Offering Practice Activities

Preview

Creating a manual that looks good to the learner is an exercise in aiding comprehension, not an exercise in aesthetics. Text that looks good helps the learner to perceive what is important and to locate information readily. Text that is clean, balanced, and thoughtfully designed is easier to read and understand than text that is cluttered, unbalanced, and haphazard.

Your goal in creating well-designed text is to have the learner say, "Wow, this is really easy to use and understand!" rather than "Wow, this is one good-looking manual!"

Here's How

To aid learner comprehension, you should present text content using:

- *Signposts* that indicate the location and relative importance of information.

- *Accessories* that make text easier to read and understand.

Offer Signposts

Think about your experience with various written materials and training sessions. Have you ever flipped through a magazine that isn't numbered on every page, for example, looking for page 89, while those special inserts dropped everywhere? Do you remember a training experience in which it was hard to figure out what was really important to know?

Difficulties like these can frustrate or alienate the learner. Avoid them by placing signposts in your manual to help the learner locate information and grasp its importance in relation to other material.

The various signposts that can be used are (1) page numbers, (2) headers or footers, (3) white space, (4) different type styles, and (5) headings and subheadings.

Here's some detailed information on how to offer signposts for the learner:

1. **Use page numbers.** Page numbers are the easiest vehicle for learners to use to find their way around a manual. If your manual has more than two pages, number them.

Earnest manual writers often needlessly complicate page numbers. The usefulness of a table of contents, an index, and directions like "See page 13" can be compromised by complex pagination schemes. Help the learner find what he or she needs by following these three rules:

◆ Keep it simple.

◆ Keep it simple.

◆ Keep it simple.

Sequential numbers like 1, 2, 3, 4, and so forth are usually best. Avoid schemes that result in page numbers like II-B-6d-23.4. Make the numbers large and visible, and put them at the top or the bottom of the page. Make sure that left pages have even numbers and right pages have odd numbers.

A generally accepted norm is to start numbering pages after the table of contents, leaving the "front matter" (the title page, the preface, and other components preceding the table of contents) without page numbers or with Roman numerals rather than Arabic numerals. It's up to you whether you follow this convention.

2. **Use *headers or footers*.** As their names imply, the signposts called "headers" and "footers" appear at the tops and bottoms of pages, respectively. The information in headers or footers helps the learner understand where he or she is and what can be found on the page.

Headers or footers also act as page borders for the learner, preventing the learner's eyes from roaming into uncharted white space and off the page.

Fill (but don't clutter) your headers or footers with details that assist the learner in locating information. Keep the content consistent from page to page. In addition to the page number, you might consider including the title of the manual, the section or module or chapter title, and/or the date of publication.

This book uses footers. The left (even-numbered) pages list page numbers plus the title of the book, and the right (odd-numbered) pages list page numbers plus the title of the module (chapter). Although this system is a common one, it's just one example of what you can do with headers or footers.

3. **Use *white space*.** White space is open space without type or figures. It's a design element that serves many functions:

◆ It helps the learner locate information and judge the importance of that information.

◆ It signals a change in activity or action.

◆ It sets off figures, tables, lists, quotes, examples, and other elements on a page.

◆ It prevents a cluttered look and aids in learner comprehension.

◆ It gives the learner a place to jot down notes and to doodle.

White space lives in the margins, in the gaps between paragraphs, between headings, around figures, and anywhere else you choose to use it. This book is a model of how much white space you should consider using; as a rough guideline, devote a third to a half of each page to white space.

Quote To Note

There's no place like white space.

A. Petit

4. **_Use different type styles for emphasis._** Certain styles of type such as _italics_, **boldface**, <u>underlining</u>, <u>double underlining</u>, outlining, shadowing, and CAPITAL LETTERS are used to <u>draw attention to</u> and _emphasize_ information. They're effective in doing so if used with RESTRAINT and applied <u>consistently</u>.

The preceding paragraph does not evidence restraint. It includes too many styles of type; it's hard to read, perplexing (in that the learner would be hard pressed to know what's important), and cluttered. Clutter impedes comprehension. Limit the use of these signposts in your manual to three or four, and exercise discretion when you use them.

Consistency in the use of type styles aids in learner understanding: If you present a new term in **boldface**, present all new terms in **boldface**; if you use _italics_ for emphasis, always use _italics_ for emphasis. Inconsistent application of type styles can confuse or distract the learner.

5. **Use *headings and subheadings*.** Headings and subheadings are handy signposts. A heading identifies a broad topic, while subheadings are smaller breakdowns of information related to a heading. Pay special attention to the amount of white space you use around headings and subheadings. Because a heading is more important than any subheading, put more white space above and below it than you put above and below subheadings.

Be consistent in the amount of white space you use in each of these four situations:

- ◆ Preceding a heading.

- ◆ Between a heading and a subheading.

- ◆ Between a heading or subheading and the text information following it.

- ◆ Between the text information belonging to one subheading and the next subheading.

In Figure 3, for example, note that there is more white space around the headings than around the subheadings. Also note that white space is consistently used throughout the figure.

Xxxxxxxxxxxxxxxxxxxxxxxxxxxxxxxxxxxxxxxxxxxxxxxxxxxxxxxxxxxxxxxx.

REVIEWING THE INVOICE (HEADING)

Checking the items (subheading)

Xxxxxxxxxxxxxxxxxxxxxxxxxxxxxxxxxxxxxxxxxxxxxxxxxxxxxxxxxxxxxxxxx
xxxxxxxxxxxxxxxxxxxxxxxxxxxxxxxxxxxxxxxxxxxxxxxxxxxxxxxxxxxxxxxxx
xxxxxxxxxxxxxxxxxxxxx.

Recalculating totals (subheading)

Xxxxxxxxxxxxxxxxxxxxxxxxxxxxxxxxxxxxxxxxxxxxxxxxxxxxxxxxxxxxxxxxx
xxxxxxxxxxxxxx.

PROCESSING THE INVOICE (HEADING)

Coding the billing number (subheading)

Xxxxxxxxxxxxxxxxxxxxxxxxxxxxxxxxxxxxxxxxxxxxxxxxxxxxxxxxxxxxxxxxx
xxxxxxxxxxxxxxxxxxxxxxxxxxxxx.

Filing (subheading)

Xxxxxxxxxxxxxxxxxxxxxxxxxxxxxxxxxxxxxxxxxxxx.

Figure 3. Spacing Around Headings and Subheadings

You can place headings and subheadings above the information they relate to, or you can place them in the margins.

Avoid too many levels of subheadings. Subheadings can spawn subheadings endlessly, creating a disturbing appearance like that shown in Figure 4. In this example it's difficult to see how information is related. Make information more accessible to the learner by limiting subheadings to two or three levels per page.

CALIBRATE THE MILLIMETER MAXIMUM (HEADING)

Set the parameters of default (first-level subheading)

Xxxxxxxxxxxxxxxxxxxxxxxxxxxxxxxxxxxxxxxxxxxxxxxxxxxxxxxxxxxxxxxxxxx xxxxxxxxxxxxxxxxxxxxxxxxxxxxxxxxxxxxxxxxxxxxxxxx.

Winch the bazooka zone fully (second-level subheading)

Xxxxxxxxxxxxxxxxxxxxxxxxxxxxxxxxxxxxxxxxxxxxxxxxxxxxxxx.

Initial the dimension of fleb (third-level subheading)

Xxxxxxxxxxxxxxxxxxxxxxxxxxxxxxxxxxxxxxxxxxxxxxxxxxxxxxxxxxxxx xxxxxxxxxxxxxxxxxxxxxxxxxxxxxxxxxxxxxx.

Advance the microdotz (fourth-level subheading)

Xxxxxxxxxxxxxxxxxxxxxxxxxxxxxxxxxxxxxxxxxxxxx.

Distill fluid (fourth-level subheading)

Xxxxxxxxxxxxxxxxxxxxxxxxxxxxxxxxxxxxxxxxxxxxxxxxxxxxx.

Winch mazooka breakage loop (second-level subheading)

Xxxxxxxxxxxxxxxxxxxxxxxxxxxxxxxxxxxxxxxxxxxxxxxxxxxxxx

Platform zamboni (fourth-level subheading)

Xxxxxxxxxxxxxxxxxxxxxxxxxxxxxxxxxxxxxxxxx.

Set dial for one thousand volts (first-level subheading)

Figure 4. Too Many Levels of Subheadings

Employ Accessories

Accessories can make thoughtfully designed content look and function better, increasing learner comprehension. But too many accessories can be distracting and can interfere with learning. When choosing accessories, choose those that foster learning, not those that obscure content. Find stylish ways to aid in comprehension.

The various accessories that can be used are (1) illustrations, (2) a suitable typeface, (3) color, (4) left-justified lines, (5) no more than one major idea per page, (6) lists, (7) tables, and (8) flow charts.

Here is some detailed information on how to employ accessories:

1. **Use illustrations liberally.** Illustrations can be sophisticated software graphics, professional works of art, or the sketchings of an amateur. Illustrations do not replace words; they supplement them. Some learners understand words better than pictures; others favor the pictures. You need to reach both types of learners.

Illustrate purposefully. Pictures that are not obviously related to the content may confuse or distract a learner.

Illustrating is an area in which you can let your imagination take flight. Consider content carefully; does anything conjure a picture that will reinforce learning? Try a few scribbles and sketches. You may discover an artistic bent you didn't know you had.

2. **Use a suitable typeface.** Select a typeface (also known as a font) that is easy to read. Research shows that *serif* typefaces, those with serifs or short strokes at the ends of the lines that make up letters, are easier to read than *sans serif* typefaces, those without serifs. Therefore, it's best to choose a serif typeface for your main text.

If you want, you may choose a sans serif typeface for headings or figures or other elements that don't call for as much continual reading as your main text. The main text in this book is set in a serif typeface called Novarese Medium; the headings and figures are set in sans serif typefaces called Kabel and Kabel Demibold. See Figure 5 for other examples of serif and sans serif typefaces.

Serif Typefaces

This is an example of Baskerville.

abcdefghijklmnopqrstuvwxyz
ABCDEFGHIJKLMNOPQRSTUVWXYZ

This is an example of Bookman Light.

abcdefghijklmnopqrstuvwxyz
ABCDEFGHIJKLMNOPQRSTUVWXYZ

This is an example of Courier.

abcdefghijklmnopqrstuvwxyz
ABCDEFGHIJKLMNOPQRSTUVWXYZ

This is an example of New Caledonia.

abcdefghijklmnopqrstuvwxyz
ABCDEFGHIJKLMNOPQRSTUVWXYZ

This is an example of Palatino Roman.

abcdefghijklmnopqrstuvwxyz
ABCDEFGHIJKLMNOPQRSTUVWXYZ

Figure 5. Samples of Serif and Sans Serif Typefaces

Sans Serif Typefaces

This is an example of Avant Garde Book.

abcdefghijklmnopqrstuvwxyz
ABCDEFGHIJKLMNOPQRSTUVWXYZ

This is an example of Eras Book.

abcdefghijklmnopqrstuvwxyz
ABCDEFGHIJKLMNOPQRSTUVWXYZ

This is an example of Futura Medium.

abcdefghijklmnopqrstuvwxyz
ABCDEFGHIJKLMNOPQRSTUVWXYZ

This is an example of Helvetica.

abcdefghijklmnopqrstuvwxyz
ABCDEFGHIJKLMNOPQRSTUVWXYZ

This is an example of Optima.

abcdefghijklmnopqrstuvwxyz
ABCDEFGHIJKLMNOPQRSTUVWXYZ

Figure 5. Samples of Serif and Sans Serif Typefaces (continued)

For use in signposts, a typeface should be variable in size (and still readable and attractive) and should have italic, bold, and bold italic variations.

3. **Use color.** Use color if your budget allows and if it will improve, not impede, learning. Within the text, use no more than two colors. To avoid budget busting, consider one color—dark blue or green ink instead of ordinary black; then use shades of blue or green for illustrations.

4. **Use left-justified lines.** According to *The Random House Dictionary* (The Unabridged Edition), justification is "the spacing of words and letters within a line of type so that all full lines in a column have even margins both on the left and on the right." This is a description of "fully justified" lines.

However, type can also be "left justified with a ragged-right margin." In this case lines begin at a particular left margin but don't end on the right at a particular point. Instead, they end on the right wherever the word-processing software logically ends them.

The text in this book is left justified with a ragged-right margin. This kind of text is especially easy to read and is what most learners are accustomed to reading. Consequently, you will probably want to make the text in your manual left justified.

5. ***Present no more than one major idea per page.*** Each time a learner turns the page, that act is a tiny mental time-out. Use this fact to the learner's benefit by presenting no more than one major idea or topic per page. For a big idea, present one or a few pieces of that idea per page. (For example, this page offers one piece of the major idea "Employ Accessories.") When you conclude an idea, consider leaving white space instead of beginning a second idea on that page. Begin another idea only if it's related to the previous one.

Quote To Note

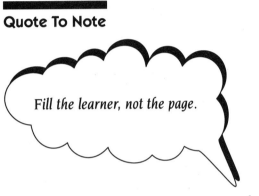

Fill the learner, not the page.

A. Petit

6. **Use lists.** When you want to present three or more related items or ideas, use a list. Lists aid in understanding because they eliminate unnecessary words and capture the essence of what the learner needs to know. You probably make lists all the time: errands to run, phone calls to make, chores to do. Grocery lists, for example, succinctly name the items to be purchased at the supermarket. It would be extremely time-consuming and hard to shop with these guidelines in place of a list:

> Stop in the produce section and pick up six bananas and four oranges. Judy wants two pineapples, too. Get three large onions— red, not white. At the deli, get a half-pound of provolone and some pepperoni.

The hapless shopper might wander among the cabbages and cantaloupes for a lot longer than necessary. Make learning faster and easier by using lists that aid in comprehension. Here are some ideas for types of lists to consider:

- ◆ Steps to take.

- ◆ Rules to follow.

- ◆ Points to remember.

- ◆ Facts to memorize.

- ◆ Characteristics to note.

You may choose to number items in a list or use a symbol or icon in front of each item. Bullets and check marks are popular for this purpose, but why not try something out of the ordinary? Be creative. Use an icon in your software or draw a symbol yourself. Be *extraordinary*.

7. **Use tables.** A particularly useful kind is known as a decision table (see the example in Table 4), because it shows a learner what to do in a given situation. Such tables are generally very simple and do a good job of promoting learning. Like lists, they present essentials with a minimum of words.

Table 4. Example of a Decision Table

IF the diagnosis is:	THEN use this code:
Migraine Headache	90046.21
Sprained Ankle	31179.455
Lower-Back Pain	55322.148
Ear Infection	10158.3

8. **Use flow charts.** A flow chart is a graphic representation of a sequence of actions. Flow charts can be helpful in simplifying information for the learner. Like lists and tables, they present the essentials with as few words as possible; when they are designed well, they are terrific learning aids. Figure 6 offers an example of an effective flow chart.

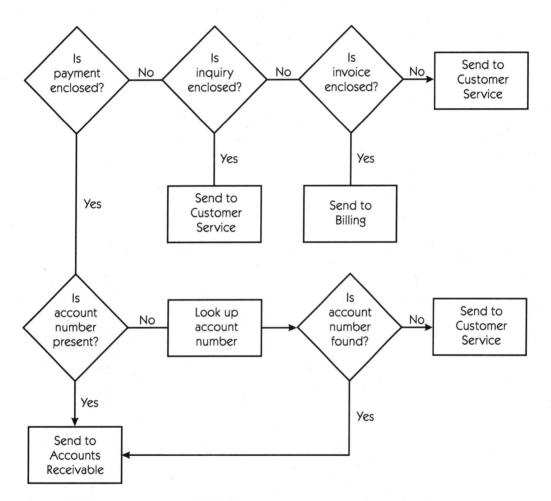

Figure 6. Example of an Effective Flow Chart (for Handling Incoming Mail)

Unfortunately, not everyone constructs flow charts in a clean, easy-to-follow manner. Some people create monstrous, multiple-page rivers of boxed words like the one shown in Figure 7. Flow charts can be very difficult to construct; remember that the purpose of a flow chart is to present information in a simple form.

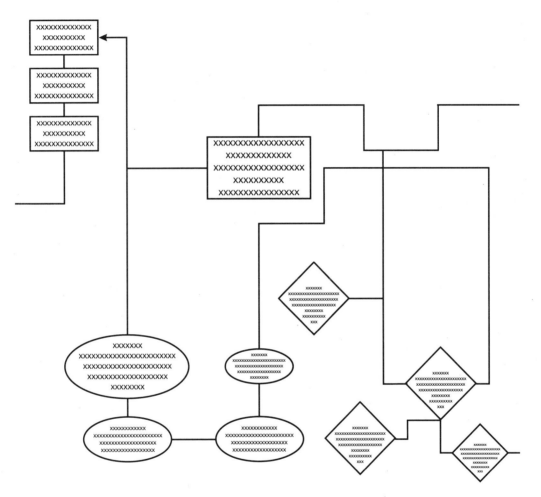

Figure 7. Example of an Ineffective Flow Chart

Highlights of This Module

By looking good, your manual will aid learner comprehension. You can make your manual look good with signposts and accessories. Signposts, which help the learner locate information and judge its relative importance, include (1) page numbers, (2) headers or footers, (3) white space, (4) different type styles (italic, bold, and so on), and (5) headings and subheadings.

Accessories, which contribute to readability and learner understanding, include (1) illustrations, (2) a suitable typeface, (3) color, (4) justified lines (left justified essential; right justified optional), (5) one major idea per page, (6) lists, (7) tables, and (8) flow charts.

Look past the ordinary. Use signposts and accessories to make your manual *extraordinary*.

Self-Check for Module 5

Take a few minutes now to assess your understanding of what looks good to the learner. Complete each of the sentences that follow. Remember that you may look back in the module if you want.

1. The easiest signpost for learners to use to find their way around a manual is:

   _____

2. Type styles are used for emphasis. To avoid distracting the learner, limit the number of type styles in a manual to:

   _____

3. Three accessories that present information with a minimum of words are:

   _____

   _____

   _____

Your Next Step

Now check your answers with those on page 94.

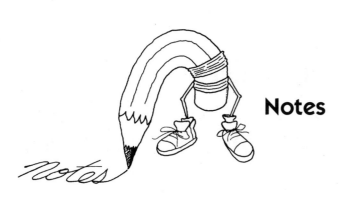

Notes

Responses to Self-Check for Module 5

Suggested responses are listed below:

1. The easiest signpost for learners to use to find their way around a manual is:

   Page numbers

2. Type styles are used for emphasis. To avoid distracting the learner, limit the number of type styles in a manual to:

   Three or four

3. Three accessories that present information with a minimum of words are:

   Lists
   Tables
   Flow charts

   How did you do? Give yourself a pat on the back for your efforts.

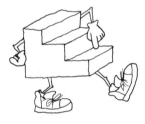

Your Next Step

Take a look at Table 5 on the next page, and use this checklist when you begin constructing a self-study manual. Then decide whether to take a break or proceed to another module.

Table 5. Looking-Good Checklist*

SIGNPOSTS AND ACCESSORIES	YES	NO**
Are pages numbered simply and visibly?		
Do headers or footers give consistent details from page to page?		
Is white space used to help locate information, signify its importance, and aid in comprehension?		
Is the white space used above and below headings and subheadings consistent?		
Are subheadings limited to two or three levels per page?		
Is the number of type styles used limited to three or four?		
Are type styles used consistently and with restraint?		
Do the illustrations reinforce the words?		
Is the text typeface easy to read and variable in size?		
Are lines left justified?		
Are major ideas limited to one per page?		
Are lists, tables, and flow charts used to minimize the need for narrative?		
** Correct any situations that caused you to answer "NO" to any question.		

Module 6

Watch Your Language: Using Friendly, Energetic, Understandable Words

Objectives; Time and Materials Required

When you've completed this module, you'll be able to do the following:

♦ Indicate whether ten statements about the language to use in a self-study manual are true or false.

Completing this module takes fifteen to thirty minutes. You'll need a pen or a pencil.

Where You Are in the Process

Section I: Preparation

- First Impression: Making Sure the Cover Beckons

- Atmospheric Conditions: Fostering a Positive Learning Environment

- An Ovation for Motivation: Offering Incentives To Learn

- Show the Way: Guiding with Clear Instructions

Section II: Presentation

- Looking Good: Using Appearance To Aid Comprehension

- **Watch Your Language: Using Friendly, Energetic, Understandable Words**

- Set the Sequence: Arranging Content for Optimal Learning

- Word Plays: Using Words Creatively To Reinforce, Emphasize, Enliven Learning

Section III: Practice

- Topple Test Tension: Dispelling Anxiety To Promote Learning

- Variety Pack: Offering Practice Activities

Preview

Many writers of self-study manuals suffer from a dread disease called "stiffosis." Once afflicted, writers use stilted language, as though their words were destined for scanning by laser beam or electronic transfer directly into the learner's brain. Complex words, awkward phrasing, and lofty language are symptoms of stiffosis.

The antidote for stiffosis is a dose of "G-E-T R-E-A-L." A self-study manual is a written conversation with the learner, so be conversational, friendly, and energetic. Seek to nurture, not numb, the learner. Acknowledge the presence and participation of the learner; put him or her at ease with easy language. In other words, watch your language!

Here's How

Here's how to "watch your language":

1. **Use conversational, everyday words.** Use words that the learner knows and understands. Here are some examples of fancy words that have plainer, more conversational substitutes:

Instead of:	Use:
utilize	use
rudimentary	simple
diminutive	small
plethora	many
pachyderm	elephant

Although fancy words can add spice to your work, too much spice can make your words unpalatable.

Quote To Note

Collect plain words and spend them wisely.

A. Petit

2. **Be concise and economical with words.** Be a word miser. You can save four words by saying "now" instead of "at this point in time."

3. **Use contractions.** Contractions are natural in conversation; they make writing informal. For example, write "you'll see" instead of "you will see" and "it won't" instead of "it will not."

4. **Address the learner as "you."** Say, "Next, you'll do a brief exercise." Talking directly to the learner is more personal than saying "Next, the learner will do a brief exercise."

5. **Review your word choices for overused, lifeless ones.** An example is "maximize," which can easily be replaced by fresh words like "enlarge," "expand," or "increase." Find a good thesaurus or a dictionary of synonyms and use it.

6. **Avoid jargon.** Jargon, also known as "bureaucratese," is like the language of a secret sect, excluding and confusing the learner. If the learner is expected to know and understand jargon on the job, and you must explain it, be sure to offer a layperson's interpretation of the jargon.

Quote To Note

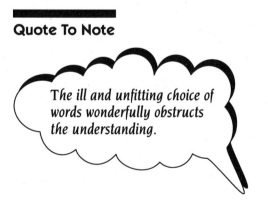

The ill and unfitting choice of words wonderfully obstructs the understanding.

Anonymous

7. **Explain the meanings of acronyms.** Acronyms are a convenient form of shorthand, but you need to explain each acronym the first time you use it. Examples include CRT for cathode ray tube and ATM for automated teller machine.

8. **Steer clear of clichés.** Clichés dull the mind. Examples include "as a matter of fact" and "it stands to reason."

9. **Construct clear, crisp sentences.** Alter the length of your sentences for variety, but always aim for brevity.

10. **Present new topics or new aspects of topics in paragraphs.** The first sentence in a paragraph identifies the topic of that paragraph for the learner. The remaining sentences should be related to the topic.

Paragraphs may be long or short, with one sentence or many. But a lengthy paragraph can induce mental paralysis, so strive for brevity without sacrificing clarity.

Review your paragraphs to make sure they are properly constructed, clear and concise. If they aren't, rewrite for clarity.

Highlights of This Module

Self-study manuals are often glazed with stilted language. Make yours sparkle with friendliness and freshness. A crisply written manual motivates the learner to keep turning the pages.

Watch your language by speaking plainly, economically, informally, and naturally. Avoid deadening language such as overused words, jargon, unexplained acronyms, and clichés. Use vivid, clear, lively language. Alter the length of your sentences for variety, but aim for brevity. Paragraphs should introduce new topics or new aspects of topics, and the shorter the better.

Rhyme Time: In the Emergency Room

I awoke in the E.R., *a nurse at my side*
To learn by stiffosis I'd been paralyzed.
Only one cure for me to better feel:
A friendly smile and a dose of G-E-T R-E-A-L.

Self-Check for Module 6

Take some time now to check your understanding of what you've read. Identify each statement as true or false by circling the "T" or the "F" preceding the statement.

T　　F　　1. A friendly, conversational tone puts a learner at ease.

T　　F　　2. Contractions are unnatural in conversation.

T　　F　　3. Dead words stimulate learning.

T　　F　　4. Jargon, when it must be learned, should be explained.

T　　F　　5. It's O.K. to use undefined acronyms.

T　　F　　6. Clichés bring freshness to self-study manuals.

T　　F　　7. Every sentence must contain six words.

T　　F　　8. The first sentence of a paragraph is the topic sentence.

T　　F　　9. A paragraph is a group of unrelated sentences.

T　　F　 10. The antidote for stiffosis is jargon.

Your Next Step

Check your responses against those on page 106.

Notes

Responses to Self-Check for Module 6

The following are responses suggested by the author:

1. A friendly, conversational tone puts a learner at ease.

   True. Write as though you're speaking directly to the learner; simple, everyday words are best.

2. Contractions are unnatural in conversation.

   False. How often have you said "Let's go" rather than "Let us go"?

3. Dead words stimulate learning.

   False. Lifeless words don't stimulate anything.

4. Jargon, when it must be learned, should be explained.

   True. Failure to explain jargon may confuse the learner.

5. It's O.K. to use undefined acronyms.

   False. Define each acronym the first time you use it.

6. Clichés bring freshness to self-study manuals.

   False. They bring staleness.

7. Every sentence must contain six words.

   False. A sentence can be of any length, but you should aim for brevity.

8. The first sentence of a paragraph is the topic sentence.

   True. It tells the learner what the paragraph is about.

9. A paragraph is a group of unrelated sentences.

   False. The sentences in a well-written paragraph are related.

10. The antidote for stiffosis is jargon.

    False. The antidote is G-E-T R-E-A-L.

   How did you do? Even if you didn't score a perfect ten, give yourself credit for your effort.

Your Next Step

Continue to another module or take a break. It's up to you.

Module 7

Set the Sequence: Arranging Content for Optimal Learning

Objectives; Time and Materials Required

When you've completed this module, you'll be able to do the following:

◆ Identify the best way to determine the order in which you present ideas in your manuals.

◆ Describe five methods for sequencing ideas.

◆ Name the method of sequencing ideas that gives the learner some control over learning.

To complete this module, you'll need a pen or a pencil and fifteen to thirty minutes.

Where You Are in the Process

Section I: Preparation

◆ First Impression: Making Sure the Cover Beckons

◆ Atmospheric Conditions: Fostering a Positive Learning Environment

◆ An Ovation for Motivation: Offering Incentives To Learn

◆ Show the Way: Guiding with Clear Instructions

Section II: Presentation

◆ Looking Good: Using Appearance To Aid Comprehension

◆ Watch Your Language: Using Friendly, Energetic, Understandable Words

 ◆ **Set the Sequence: Arranging Content for Optimal Learning**

◆ Word Plays: Using Words Creatively To Reinforce, Emphasize, Enliven Learning

Section III: Practice

◆ Topple Test Tension: Dispelling Anxiety To Promote Learning

◆ Variety Pack: Offering Practice Activities

Preview

Presenting training content in a logical order allows you to build a framework of knowledge that expands from fundamentals to full mastery. There are many alternatives for sequencing your material. The thrust here is to show you the options; the content and intent of your instruction will determine which alternative, or combination of alternatives, works best for your manual.

The first step to take in deciding on the content sequence is to do an outline of the entire manual. You probably did one when you decided on the contents of your manual. If not, you need to do one now. Once you have the entire contents set out, you can begin to determine order.

Choose the content sequence that is most conducive to learning the material being presented.

Here's How

Select from these methods for ordering the content of your manual. If these methods don't work for you, feel free to invent your own, as long as they make learning easy for the learner.

1. **A to Z.** If there are skills or knowledge that the learner will later use in a prescribed sequence, *then* train in the prescribed step-by-step sequence.

For example, someone learning data entry needs to key information in a certain order. Sequence the learning to duplicate the way in which that learning will be applied later.

2. ***Common to less common.*** If there are skills or knowledge that the learner will use more often than others, place them first; *then* present the rest.

For example, a clerk spends 70 percent of his or her time processing invoices and 30 percent distributing material. Give learning about invoices top billing.

3. ***Simple to complex.*** If there are skills and knowledge that are easier to master than others, *then* present them first as a foundation of knowledge—as well as a source of early success.

For example, a student chef needs to know how to properly core tomatoes before he or she learns how to stuff them.

4. **Known to unknown.** If the learner already has a basic understanding, *then* refresh his or her knowledge and move on.

For example, let's assume that a learner who speaks Spanish needs to master French. In your manual you would point out and capitalize on the similarities of the two languages in order to build a foundation of what is already understood and to make the learner feel comfortable.

5. **One to another.** If the learner can learn skills in any order, *then* give him or her the choice.

For example, in *Secrets To Enliven Learning*, you can do the modules within each section in whatever order you choose. Each module stands alone and is not dependent for clarity on the modules preceding it. As the learner, you're in control. Offer your learners this same control whenever possible.

Rhyme Time

Right, left, back and forth,
East, west, south and north—
Choices for order are more than a few;
The one for your manual is up to you.

Highlights of This Module

The best way to decide how to order your manual is to do an outline. Once the contents of the manual are known, you can choose from at least five methods of order. You can use combinations as well. There are no rigid rules about the order in which material is presented; the content and intent of instruction, along with your best judgment, are factors in the decision. Set your sights on a sequence that will yield *extraordinary* results.

Self-Check for Module 7

Take a moment to check what you've just read. You can review the text for help in answering these questions, but first try it on your own. You may come up with some imaginative responses in addition to the ones presented in this module.

1. What is the first step to take in deciding on the content sequence of your manual?

_____

2. What are five alternatives for putting ideas in order?

_____

_____

_____

_____

3. Which method for putting ideas in order enables the learner to exercise some control over learning?

_____

Your Next Step

Check your responses against those on page 116.

Responses to Self-Check for Module 7

The following are recommended responses. Congratulate yourself if you came up with these answers plus some additional imaginative responses.

1. What is the first step to take in deciding on the content sequence of your manual?

   Do an outline.

2. What are five alternatives for putting ideas in order?

   A to Z
   Common to less common
   Simple to complex
   Known to unknown
   One to another

3. Which method for putting ideas in order enables the learner to exercise some control over learning?

   One to another

   Not too bad, was it? It's clear that deciding on the order of presentation is an inexact process that must be tailored to the content and intent of your instruction.

Your Next Step

Look at Table 6 on the next page. Use this Learning-Sequence Decision Table to help you decide on a learning sequence once you've done an outline. Then begin another module if you wish.

Table 6. Learning-Sequence Decision Table*

IF	THAT	THEN
There are skills or bits of knowledge	the learner uses in a prescribed order	train in a step-by-step sequence
	the learner uses more often than others	present them before those that are used less frequently
	are easier to master than others	present them first
	the learner basically understands	refresh knowledge and move on
	can be learned in any order	give the learner the choice of order

*This table may be freely reproduced for educational/training activities. There is no requirement to obtain special permission for such uses. Please make sure that the following statement appears on all reproductions:

Module 8

Word Plays: Using Words Creatively To Reinforce, Emphasize, Enliven Learning

Objectives; Time and Materials Required

When you've completed this module, you'll be able to do the following:

- ◆ Create a short rhyme.
- ◆ Compose a metaphor.
- ◆ Write a brief summary of what you learned in this module.
- ◆ List the three most effective word plays.

To complete this module, you'll need a pen or a pencil and one to two hours.

Where You Are in the Process

Section I: Preparation

- First Impression: Making Sure the Cover Beckons

- Atmospheric Conditions: Fostering a Positive Learning Environment

- An Ovation for Motivation: Offering Incentives To Learn

- Show the Way: Guiding with Clear Instructions

Section II: Presentation

- Looking Good: Using Appearance To Aid Comprehension

- Watch Your Language: Using Friendly, Energetic, Understandable Words

- Set the Sequence: Arranging Content for Optimal Learning

- **Word Plays: Using Words Creatively To Reinforce, Emphasize, Enliven Learning**

Section III: Practice

- Topple Test Tension: Dispelling Anxiety To Promote Learning

- Variety Pack: Offering Practice Activities

Preview

Think about the ways you learned as a child. Rhymes and stories and songs were probably a big part of your experience; no doubt you recall singing the alphabet and listening to stories. Don't worry—you won't be singing a training ballad next. But you will apply your childhood learning along with grown-up methods to enliven your self-study manuals.

Although a picture may be worth a thousand words, there are other ways to boost the value of words. The word plays described in this module do not replace narrative; they reinforce and emphasize it. Use word plays to help the learner learn.

Here's How

Here's how to play with words creatively:

1. **Use rhyme.** When's a good time for a rhyme? Any time at all! Consider one important idea that you want to emphasize, and give yourself some time to play around with words that express that idea. There's no need to write an epic; two or four short lines will do.

Use a thesaurus to find a good rhyming word. For example, you might want to make a rhyme about a rodent. Although the word "rodent" might seem at first to have limited rhyming potential, you might look up "rodent" in a thesaurus and find "rat," which offers a gold mine of rhyme:

> *I had a rat, it ate my hat,*
> *and so I sat and squashed it flat.*

Find a rhyming dictionary at a bookstore. Or use the low-budget "run-through-the-alphabet approach," which works like this:

able...bable...cable...dable...eable...fable...and so on.

Here's another simple rhyme:

> *My rhymes are fine*
> *and so sublime,*
> *My learners find*
> *them most divine.*

Relax with it, and you'll find that it'll come to you. Unleash your creativity; you'll be surprised and pleased with what you can do.

2. **Use metaphors.** What's a metaphor for? A metaphor is a figure of speech that compares one object to another, implying a similarity between two essentially different things:

- ◆ "The self-study manual was a beacon of light for learners in the dark."

Metaphors use words to compose images. When you read the example of a metaphor, did your mind rapidly draw a picture of a beacon? Probably! Metaphors are a great way to plant an image in the mind of a learner.

Here are two other examples:

- ◆ "The training certificate is a passport to success."
- ◆ "The manager's grin was a stamp of approval."

Exercise Your Mind

Try writing your own metaphors:

A sunny day is_____

_____.

This module is_____.

_____.

3. **Use similes.** Is a simile similar to a metaphor? Very! A simile is just like a metaphor except that it includes the word "as" or the word "like": "The self-study manual was *like* a beacon of light for learners in the dark." A simile identifies common characteristics of unlike things.

Here are some more examples:

- "He's as busy as a bee."

- "She's as sharp as a tack."

- "I'm as hungry as a tiger."

Exercise Your Mind

Take a second to turn the metaphors you wrote into similes.

A sunny day is_____

_____.

This module is_____

_____.

A special note: True word misers always favor metaphor over simile. Why? Because it saves at least one word ("like" or "as") per figure of speech!

4. **Use examples.** An example is quite substantial! An example in a self-study manual shows a learner "what a good one looks like." It serves as a model for the learner to imitate, just as *Secrets To Enliven Learning* serves as a model for you to imitate when you develop your own self-study manuals. Examples reinforce and clarify learning.

There are two types of examples: realistic and fanciful.

For example, imagine that in your manual you must describe a computer screen the learner will use. Show the screen in your manual, and be sure it's completed, not blank. That's a *realistic* example.

Now imagine that you have to explain the structure of a large airline. You could use that most exhausted name, ABC Company, or you could wax whimsical and call your airline Intergalactic Airways. That's a *fanciful* example.

Use ample examples. After presenting a new concept or skill, ask yourself if an example would clarify that concept or skill for the learner. Always provide examples of forms, checks, screens, or other items that the learner will use.

5. **Use acronyms.** What's an acronym, anyway? An acronym is a word formed from the first letter of several other words. An example is HOMES, which stands for the five North American Great Lakes: <u>H</u>uron, <u>O</u>ntario, <u>M</u>ichigan, <u>E</u>rie, and <u>S</u>uperior.

When you want learners to memorize a list, search for an acronym.

Here's an example in which the steps in a process are structured into an acronym:

Step 1: <u>R</u>un a printout of program.

Step 2: <u>A</u>ttach the specs to the program.

Step 3: <u>N</u>ote error messages on the printout.

Step 4: <u>C</u>hange the parameters to highlight errors.

Step 5: <u>H</u>ighlight the new parameters.

Step 6: <u>E</u>stimate the time to correct errors.

Step 7: <u>S</u>ubmit to manager for approval.

Although this acronym may not be the world's best, the learner may be able to recall these steps by thinking of the acronym RANCHES.

6. **Use quotes.** Should you vote for a quote? Aye! Quotes are useful for emphasis. They should be clearly related to the topic or idea at hand. Libraries have books of quotations; find one that suits you. You won't find a book entitled *Training Quotes for Today*, but you can search your own imagination for a few words that succinctly make your point. Aristotle, Mark Twain, and other quotable people don't have the market cornered. Make up a pithy saying or two. Who says you can't?

Here are two quotes. One was fashioned by a certifiable genius, the other by an ordinary sort with an average IQ. Can you pick the words of a genius?

◆ "Imagination is more important than knowledge."

◆ "Imagination is mightier than the mightiest intellect."

If you picked the first one, you get the Albert Einstein Award for Good Guessing (AEAGG). If you picked the second one, thanks from an average IQ!

Exercise Your Mind

Take a few moments to frame your own quotable quote about imagination.

Imagination is_____

_____.

7. **Use stories.** Will a story bring you glory? Probably not. But stories that are vivid and meaningful are effective learning tools. They can inspire, inform, entertain. And, as every parent knows, they can even enchant. Consider telling a story whenever you want to emphasize learning by placing it in a familiar context for the learner.

For example, if you want to illustrate how your company serves customers, tell a story about one customer's experience. Bring the customer and your company alive for the learner; depict various departments as they act and react. Make it real. Use your story to make a positive statement about your company.

Or use a story about quality to drive home your company's commitment to "doing it right the first time." Find a situation in which quality was delivered despite overwhelming obstacles. Relate quality on a personal level that the learner can readily digest and understand.

In writing your story, keep these guidelines in mind:

- ◆ Decide on a theme, and weave it into the fabric of your story.

- ◆ Keep the story short and simple.

- ◆ Use active verbs and vivid adjectives to help the learner "see" the story.

- ◆ Populate your story with characters who are familiar and believable.

- ◆ Use dialogue that sounds like conversation, not speech making.

- ◆ Create a sense of time and place. Is the story unfolding in the present? Are the characters at work?

- ◆ Animate. Make things happen!

8. **Use questions.** Should you be leery of a query? Certainly not! Questions not only spur the learner into bringing his or her own knowledge and experience into the learning process, but also give the learner a chance to mull over new material. Your intent is to stimulate thought and review.

You're right if you're thinking that some learners won't answer the questions posed. There's nothing you can do about that. If you've done everything you can to motivate the learner, and the learner understands that he or she is in charge, you must trust the learner to do what needs to be done. So don't worry about it.

Here are examples of questions:

◆ A question such as the following asks the learner to add his or her experience to the learning: "What other sorts of word plays have you used in your training?"

◆ A question like this one allows the learner to pause and consider what he or she has learned: "In what other situations would this approach work?"

9. **Use reviews.** What's the news on frequent reviews? Summarizing learning at regular intervals throughout your self-study manual reinforces learning and spotlights what is most important for the learner. Summaries are short and concise and are often presented as outlines rather than complete sentences. Follow these basics in creating summaries:

◆ Construct a sentence or phrase that succinctly captures the essence of each item you want the learner to remember.

◆ Plant the summary at the end of a module, section, chapter or whatever you're calling the smallest structural breakdown of your self-study manual.

◆ Place the summary before any practice activities.

Be *extraordinary* in labeling your summary; give it a name that's lively (as well as identifiable as what it is), such as "One More Time!," "The Last Word," or "Highlights."

10. **Use mental imagery.** It's the ultimate word play—it eliminates words entirely! Mental imagery is a way of guiding the learner into visualizing a situation in a positive way. It is often used to allow the learner to see himself or herself in action, successfully using a new skill or knowledge.

Athletes use mental imagery to help them overcome anxiety, to perfect a pitch or a golf stroke. When you use mental imagery, you consciously create a scene in your mind that is as real as what your eyes might see. Your mind perceives the scene as real and reacts emotionally.

You may already use mental imagery. It lives under many names: visioning, positive imagery, end-result imagery, mental rehearsal, and others. If you think of mental imagery as mental rehearsal, then it's easy to see how such rehearsal can affect real performance.

Try this mental-imagery exercise:

> Imagine that you're a customer-service representative learning how to deal with difficult customers. Picture this situation:
>
> The phone rings. You answer as you normally do, pleasantly and with a helpful tone. The caller yells, "You really messed up this time! If I get one more bill from you morons...."
>
> See yourself remaining calm and listening to the customer. Notice how your posture is erect and your pen is poised. The look on your face betrays no tension, just a jaw set in concentration and a desire to take care of this customer. Your voice is level and controlled as you begin to ask for information and soothe the customer's anger.
>
> At the end of the conversation, the customer is placated and accepts your sincere apology. You say good-bye and hang up the receiver gently. You take a deep breath, write a few notes, and the phone rings....

If you're new to the idea of mental imagery, you may be skeptical. But try it yourself. The next time you're anxious about performing—whether that's speaking in public, pitching an inning, or giving bad news to your manager—picture that performance in your mind in a positive way.

Envision every aspect of the situation: your surroundings; the people who are present; how you look, sound, and move. See your performance unfold and conclude successfully. Your speech was enthusiastically received, you pitched a no-hitter, the boss understood. When it's time for the actual performance, it will seem very comfortable and familiar to you. Your anxiety will be low because you've rehearsed the situation before in your mind. You might not necessarily be perfect, but you'll be better than you would have been otherwise. So let it happen. You'll "see"!

Highlights of This Module

Use words imaginatively to sustain the learner's interest. Rhymes, figures of speech, examples, acronyms, questions, examples, quotes, stories, reviews or summaries, and mental imagery add the variety and freshness that create *extraordinary* learning experiences.

Self-Check for Module 8

This self-check is different from the others you've completed. You'll need a decent chunk of time, perhaps an hour, to see how well you can apply what you've just read. Have fun with this; challenge your creativity and imagination. See if being *extraordinary* isn't a lot more fun (and, yes, more work) than being ordinary.

1. Write a two-hundred-word summary of what you've learned in this module.

2. Write a four-line rhyme about your car.

_____

_____

_____

_____

3. Write a metaphor about your home.

_____

_____

4. In your opinion, which of the word plays covered in this module are the three most effective?

_____

_____

_____

This time you're on your own. There are no suggested responses from the author. Your effort and imagination enabled you to see what is possible. Keep looking within. Creativity and inventiveness are locked inside you—let them out!

Section III:

Practice

Module 9

Topple Test Tension: Dispelling Anxiety To Promote Learning

Objectives; Time and Materials Required

When you've completed this module, you'll be able to do the following:

- ◆ Select ways to reduce test tension.

- ◆ Identify guidelines for giving practice answers.

- ◆ Choose the information to include in learner instructions.

To complete this module, you'll need a pen or a pencil and about an hour.

Where You Are in the Process

Section I: Preparation

◆ First Impression: Making Sure the Cover Beckons

◆ Atmospheric Conditions: Fostering a Positive Learning Environment

◆ An Ovation for Motivation: Offering Incentives To Learn

◆ Show the Way: Guiding with Clear Instructions

Section II: Presentation

◆ Looking Good: Using Appearance To Aid Comprehension

◆ Watch Your Language: Using Friendly, Energetic, Understandable Words

◆ Set the Sequence: Arranging Content for Optimal Learning

◆ Word Plays: Using Words Creatively To Reinforce, Emphasize, Enliven Learning

Section III: Practice

◆ **Topple Test Tension: Dispelling Anxiety To Promote Learning**

◆ Variety Pack: Offering Practice Activities

Preview

Have you ever become tense and anxious before taking a test, whether it was a math test, a driving test, or an IQ test? If so, you're not alone. Thousands of learners get moist palms at the mention of the word "test." It conjures many emotions, most of them negative. Yet testing, or practice, is the only way to measure mastery and make the learner a full participant in learning.

Practice is *doing*, whether it's processing a practice invoice, composing a sample letter, or answering a potential customer question. Doing includes such tasks as defining a term, selecting from a list of items, and building a model.

Quote To Note

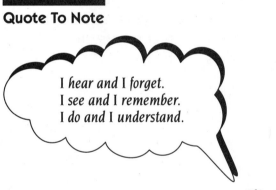

I *hear* and I *forget*.
I *see* and I *remember*.
I *do* and I *understand*.

Chinese proverb

Practice should measure learning in a way that reduces test tension, allows self-evaluation, instills confidence, and encourages effort. The learner who doesn't feel threatened or intimidated by tests approaches practice as a chance to measure what he or she has learned without fear of failure.

Topple the learner's tension!

Here's How

Here's how to dispel anxiety:

1. ***Say that mistakes are* O.K.** Early in your self-study manual, let the learner know that it's O.K. to make mistakes. Encourage the learner who stumbles to get up and try again; make getting up easy by judging gently.

Perfection is a goal that is sometimes out of reach, but you're right if you're thinking that sometimes you must insist on perfection. In matters of life and death, such as microscopic brain surgery and nuclear power generation, stumbling is discouraged. When lives are at stake, consider a learning method other than self-study. When dignity is at stake, consider stumbling as just one step to mastery.

2. ***Play the name game.*** When you need to measure learning, offer a practice that allows the learner to show what he or she can do, but avoid the "T" word ("test"). Instead, use a euphemism that blunts the edge of anxiety. Here are some alternative names for "test":

- ◆ Self-check (the term that's used in this book).

- ◆ Self-appraisal.

- ◆ Self-assessment.

These labels are sufficient to reduce test tension, but there's opportunity here to go beyond the ordinary and reach for the *extraordinary*. Use your imagination to think of a name that overcomes anxiety with playful familiarity. For example, if your manual has to do with athletics, call your practices "instant replays" or "warmups." If your manual has to do with the theatrical world, call your practices "rehearsals" or "tryouts."

3. **Express confidence in the learner's ability.** Anticipate that every learner will succeed. You might say something like "Take a few moments now to check your progress by responding to the statements below. Relax and give it your best. You can do it."

4. **Create realistic conditions.** Set practice conditions that parallel what the learner will find on the job. Are references used on the job? Then allow them to be used during practice. Can the learner consult with others at work? Then allow consultation during practice.

Avoid creating the kind of artificial testing atmosphere that you may remember from school, when you probably heard something like this: "All books off your desks! Eyes on your papers! Quiet! Begin!"

Try instead, "It's O.K. to go back through the text or use the references on the bookshelf. Collaborate with another learner if you like."

5. **Broaden your definition of a correct answer.** You may be used to practice situations in which there are defined and inflexibly correct answers. For some training, that's necessary. For example, in the nuclear-power industry, coming close to choosing the correct button to press is not good enough.

However, in many kinds of training it's possible to allow for learner responses that are more than rote statements culled from the manual. Critical thinking and imagination can produce inventive, fresh responses. Of course, you want the learner to glean information from your manual, but don't limit the learner to what you know to be correct. Trust the learner to be able to have some ideas of his or her own.

Foster creative, *extraordinary* intellectual activity.

Instead of giving answers labeled as "correct," give "suggested," "possible," "reasonable," or "the author's" responses, and give extra credit for independent, imaginative responses.

6. **Have the answers available.** Provide an answer sheet so that the learner can check his or her work. If you choose self-study as a learning method, use self-assessment as your practice method.

7. **Acknowledge extraordinary performance with liberal praise.** You might say, "If you matched all ten correctly, terrific! You'll have no trouble negotiating new sales contracts!" Put yourself in the learner's place. An expression of praise is recognition of achievement that's hard to come by in a self-study approach.

Quote To Note

> It is a great sign of mediocrity to praise always moderately.

Vauvenargues

8. **Encourage the learner who stumbles.** Think about what you might say to a friend who clipped a curb and fell trying in-line skates for the first time. You'd offer comfort and encouragement, right? Do the same for the learner.

For example, you might say, "If you didn't get all of the responses, give yourself a pat on the back for trying. Consider trying again; everything you need is in the module. Go for it!"

9. **Give clear instructions.** Clear directions avoid the uneasiness that comes with not understanding what to do. At least tell the learner the following:

◆ What materials he or she will need to complete the practice (forms, calculators, and so on).

◆ Whether or not the practice is "open book." (In self-study, this should always be the case.)

◆ What to do when he or she has completed the practice (checking answers, continuing in the text, or taking a break).

Always strive to topple test tension in order to foster success.

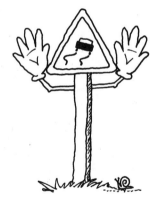

Caution!

It's natural for you, as the writer of your manual, to assume that your set of instructions is clear and complete. It probably is, but confirm the presumed clarity and completeness by trying your practice on a willing colleague, making sure the instructions lead him or her to do exactly what you intend for the learner to do.

Highlights of This Module

Express confidence in the learner; let him or her know that it's O.K. to stumble. Encourage the learner to get up and try again, and praise generously. Give your practice a nonthreatening, playful name, avoiding the "T word." Make practice as realistic as possible, and offer clear instructions. Have the practice answers nearby for the learner. Encourage the learner to think creatively and look beyond what's in your manual; modify your view of "correct" answers accordingly. You'll find that the results can be *extraordinary*.

Exercise Your Mind

Before completing the self-check for this module, consider participating in a short songfest. Read the words below as a rhyme, sing them softly under your breath, or belt them out while driving.

Don't Give Me a Test
(Sung to the tune of "Home on the Range")

Don't give me a test, 'cause I'm not at my best
When test tension has gripped me too tight—
But give me some fun, soon I'll be number one,
And my answers will always be right.
Test, test, want to flee
When a test in a module I see
So give me some play, 'cause I want a new way
To check on my learning today.

Self-Check for Module 9

Take just a minute now to check your understanding of what you've just read. For each of the multiple-choice items below, circle one or more responses.

1. When naming a practice, remember that:

    ◆ The "T" word may make a learner anxious.

    ◆ An imaginative, familiar name as a substitute for the "T" word makes the learner less anxious.

    ◆ Neither of the above.

2. When providing the practice answers:

    ◆ Always have a set of rigidly correct answers.

    ◆ Don't trust the learner to have his or her own thoughts.

    ◆ Neither of the above.

3. Instructions to the learner should include:

    ◆ What materials are needed.

    ◆ What to do when practice has been completed.

    ◆ Neither of the above.

Your Next Step

Check your responses with those on page 148.

Responses to Self-Check for Module 9

The following are suggested responses to the self-check:

1. When naming a practice, remember that:

   - The "T" word may make a learner anxious.

   - An imaginative, familiar name as a substitute for the "T" word makes the learner less anxious.

   - Neither of the above.

2. When providing the practice answers:

   - Always have a set of rigidly correct answers.

   - Don't trust the learner to have his or her own thoughts.

   - Neither of the above.

   Instead, foster critical thinking and imaginative responses. Encourage the learner to come up with his or her own ideas.

3. Instructions to the learner should include:

   - What materials are needed.

   - What to do when practice has been completed.

   - Neither of the above.

   How did you do? Be sure to congratulate yourself for your efforts!

Your Next Step

If you haven't done the next module, keep going. You've almost completed the book!

Module 10

Variety Pack: Offering Practice Activities

Objectives; Time and Materials Required

When you've completed this module, you'll be able to do the following:

- ◆ Name three practice methods that elicit guess answers.

- ◆ Identify four practice methods from brief descriptions.

To complete this module, you'll need a pen or a pencil and thirty to forty-five minutes.

Where You Are in the Process

Section I: Preparation

◆ First Impression: Making Sure the Cover Beckons

◆ Atmospheric Conditions: Fostering a Positive Learning Environment

◆ An Ovation for Motivation: Offering Incentives To Learn

◆ Show the Way: Guiding with Clear Instructions

Section II: Presentation

◆ Looking Good: Using Appearance To Aid Comprehension

◆ Watch Your Language: Using Friendly, Energetic, Understandable Words

◆ Set the Sequence: Arranging Content for Optimal Learning

◆ Word Plays: Using Words Creatively To Reinforce, Emphasize, Enliven Learning

Section III: Practice

◆ Topple Test Tension: Dispelling Anxiety To Promote Learning

◆ **Variety Pack: Offering Practice Activities**

Preview

There are many ways to practice, even in a self-study environment. The same type of practice, supplied over and over, numbs the learner. Avoid practice paralysis by choosing an assortment of practice methods from the "variety pack."

Practice is an area in which your imagination can really soar. Use your creative powers to find innovative ways to provide practice; put a little play into practice without overshadowing its intent.

Here's How

To include a variety of practice activities in your manual, consider using these methods:

1. **Short-answer questions.** Such questions can usually be answered in one sentence or a short list, for example, "What are the three principles of adult learning?"

2. **Learner summaries.** These are learner-constructed summaries of material. Asking the learner to write such a summary gives him or her a chance to express what has just been learned, for example, "Take about three minutes now to summarize what you've read in the past six pages."

3. **Essay questions.** These questions are useful when judging critical thinking, and in finding out whether the learner can assemble large amounts of learning into a cohesive whole. Use them sparingly, but use them, as in "Compare self-study programs with classroom learning, citing the advantages and disadvantages of each to the developer and the learner."

4. **Fill in the blank.** This approach is a short answer phrased as a statement rather than a question, as in "The three principles of adult learning are _____, _____, and _____."

5. **True or false.** True-or-false practice is popular with learners, as they have a 50/50 chance of being correct, whether by knowledge or guesswork.

Use of true-or-false statements can be effective but should be limited. Construct true-or-false statements carefully. You can write statements that are very true or very false, or you can use a little bit of gray to stimulate thinking. Avoid tricky true-or-false statements; they can leave the learner feeling duped.

Be sure to explain true-or-false answers fully. The learner wants not only the right answers, but also why the statements are true or false.

6. **Matching.** This kind of practice asks the learner to match one set of items to a corresponding set of answers. Try this example:

Match the former presidents of the United States with a related accomplishment or place by drawing an arrow from the name on the left to the phrase on the right.

A. George Washington	San Juan Hill
B. James Monroe	Delaware River
C. Theodore Roosevelt	Monticello
D. Thomas Jefferson	Monroe Doctrine

(The answer is on page 160.)

Matching tends to foster guesswork. Once the learner has paired the items he or she knows, a random match of the leftovers follows. So match judiciously.

7. **Multiple choice.** In this type of practice, three or four potentially correct answers are listed and the learner is asked to choose among them. Try this example:

Circle the capital of the United States:

A. Washington, CT

B. Mount Washington

C. Washington, DC

D. Washington Machine

(The answer is on page 160.)

Two of the answers are often very similar, so that they will be thought provoking to the learner. As is the case with true-or-false practice, multiple choice can be perceived as tricky by the learner.

8. *Case study*. A case study relates a detailed situation to the learner, who is asked to analyze the case and decide on a course of action. Case study is often used in courses on negotiation or sales, when many variables govern the determination of an appropriate action.

Stop just a moment, please. Which of the practice methods you've read about so far might measure good guessing as opposed to learning?

1._____

2._____

3._____

You're right if you said true or false, matching, and multiple choice.

The practice methods noted so far may be very familiar to you; they are ordinary, everyday approaches. Now it's time to get *extraordinary*. It's possible to approach practice with a sense of playfulness that doesn't obscure the purpose. Here are a few examples of what you can consider providing in the way of practice opportunities:

9. *Learner speaks*. With this approach the learner is asked to add what he or she knows to what has been taught, for example, "What else could the trainer have done to set up practice?"

10. *Job aids*. This kind of practice involves asking the learner to construct reference material on the training topic. The job aid is intended as a means of simplifying an idea or task; it serves both as a review mechanism and later as an on-the-job reference.

11. *Crossword puzzles*. These aren't much different from short-answer questions. You just ask the learner to write his or her answer in little squares.

12. **"Word find."** This approach is a short-answer question in which the answer is concealed in a square full of letters. The answer (a word) may be presented horizontally, vertically, diagonally, or backward. The learner needs to find it.

Try this example:

FRUITFIND

1. Varieties of this fruit include McIntosh, Granny Smith, and Delicious.

2. This citrus fruit has a color for a name.

3. This fuzz-covered delight is grown in the U.S. in the state of Georgia.

4. This long, yellow fruit comes in bunches.

M	K	G	I	H	O	L
S	R	B	C	R	N	Q
U	V	A	A	W	Z	A
E	E	N	P	B	J	L
P	G	A	C	P	D	F
E	N	N	Y	U	L	I
P	G	A	K	A	M	E

(The answer is on page 160.)

13. **Word scrambles.** With this kind of practice, you give the learner the correct answer, but the letters are scrambled.

Try this example:

This city is known as the City of Brotherly Love:

LAAPPIDHHILE

(The answer is on page 161.)

14. **Word jumbles.** Word jumbles go a step beyond word scrambles. The learner is asked a few questions, and the answers are given in scrambled form. The learner unscrambles the letters and writes them in boxes in which selected letters of those answers have been precircled. The learner then uses the circled letters to create a word or words that answer another question.

Try this example:

JUNGLE JUMBLE

1. The animal called "King of the Jungle."

NLOI

2. Where the King lives.

RALI

3. Tarzan's significant other.

NEJA

4. Tarzan's chimpanzee pet.

TACHEEH

5. The name of Tarzan's foundling son.

OYB

Final Question: What skimpy clothing did Tarzan wear?

_____

(The answers are on page 161.)

15. **Connect the dots.** This practice is usually seen in coloring books and other children's activity books. You may think that connecting the dots has no place in adult learning, but think again. What if the answer you were looking for could be depicted graphically? Yes, a whole quiz based on connecting the dots may not work, but consider using it in the text for some variety.

16. **Collaboration.** In a self-study environment, collaboration is not only possible but desirable. To check the learner's understanding, ask the learner to relate what he or she has learned to someone else. The collaborator's questions help clarify and confirm mastery. Encourage the learner to show off new knowledge or skill.

The collaborator may be anyone: a coworker, a friend, a family member. A learner without a partner can receive some of the same benefits by speaking into an audiotape machine and then replaying the result.

Exercise Your Mind

Try collaborating now. Decide which three practice methods will be most effective in your self-study manual. Write them here:

_____

_____

_____

Next, find a colleague or friend and ask if he or she has a few minutes. Describe the three practice methods for your collaborator, and explain how you'll apply them. When you've finished, consider whether the effort helped clarify your selections and your thinking. It probably did. You also may have enhanced the descriptions in this module with your own.

Then continue reading in the module.

You may be thinking, "This is silly stuff. Learners won't buy it. I don't buy it." You could be right. Some learners cling to more traditional, ordinary approaches, and there's nothing wrong with that. But many others will respond positively and join in with a sense of play. Why not take a chance? Try your hand at innovative ways to bring playfulness to learning, and test the results with a collaborator. You may be pleasantly surprised at the outcome.

Quote To Note

People do not quit playing because they grow old. They grow old because they quit playing.

Oliver Wendell Holmes
(who played until his death
at age ninety-three!)

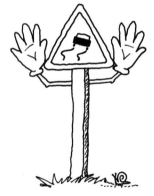

Caution!

Despite your best efforts at bringing play into learning, it won't appeal to some learners. So be sure to retain the active participation of less willing learners by not going overboard.

Offer alternatives to the playful approaches. For example, if you choose to do a "word find," you could offer the learner two options: one to write the answer on an answer sheet and a second to locate the answer within the "word find" square.

Highlights of This Module

Give the learner a variety of ways to practice. Among the best from this variety pack are (1) short-answer questions, (2) learner summaries, (3) fill in the blank, (4) learner speaks, (5) job aids, (6) crossword puzzles, (7) word scrambles, (8) word jumbles, and (9) collaboration. Use your imaginative powers to create *extraordinary* practice methods.

Practice Answers

Matching Answer:

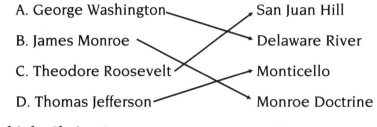

A. George Washington   San Juan Hill

B. James Monroe   Delaware River

C. Theodore Roosevelt   Monticello

D. Thomas Jefferson   Monroe Doctrine

Multiple-Choice Answer:

A. Washington, CT

B. Mount Washington

C. Washington, DC

D. Washington Machine

FRUITFIND Answer:

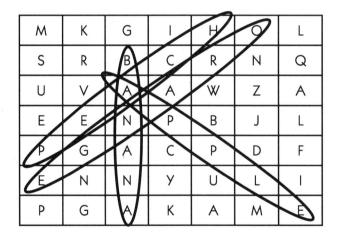

Word-Scramble Answer: Philadelphia

Jungle-Jumble Answers:

1. The animal called "King of the Jungle": LION

2. Where the King lives: LAIR

3. Tarzan's significant other: JANE

4. Tarzan's chimpanzee pet: CHEETAH

5. The name of Tarzan's foundling son: BOY

What skimpy clothing did Tarzan wear? LOINCLOTH

Self-Check for Module 10

It's time to assess what you've learned. Write your answers in the blanks provided, or try the word-jumble approach. It's up to you.

1. Name the practice method (two words) in which the learner constructs reference material.

   DOJBAI _____ _____

2. Name the type of practice (two words) in which the learner is given a detailed situation and asked to indicate what action he or she would take.

   TUSDYEACS _____ _____

3. This practice method (three words) gives the learner a 50/50 chance of getting the correct answer.

   SRRALFEOEUT _____ ____ _____

4. Name the practice (two words) that asks the learner to select from a list of possible answers.

   LIITPUMELOCCHE _____ _____

   You can stop here and check your work with the responses on page 163, or you can take the circled letters from your answers above and try to figure out the exclamation they form:

Now check your work with the answers on page 163.

Responses to Self-Check for Module 10

The following are suggested responses. If you came up with additional, creative responses, good for you!

1. Name the practice method (two words) in which the learner constructs reference material.

   Job Aid

2. Name the type of practice (two words) in which the learner is given a detailed situation and asked to indicate what action he or she would take.

   Case Study

   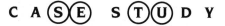

3. This practice method (three words) gives the learner a 50/50 chance of getting the correct answer.

   True or False

4. Name the practice (two words) that asks the learner to select from a list of possible answers.

   Multiple Choice

   The exclamation:

   J B I S E T U T R O A E M U T L H E

   It's a jumble out there!

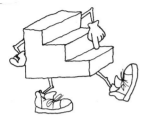

Your Next Step

Depending on the order in which you read the modules in this section, you may or may not have completed this book. If you've read the entire book, you've covered all of the essentials for developing effective self-study manuals with a touch of creativity and whimsy. Have fun with your manuals!

Bibliography

Blank, W.E. (1982). *Handbook for developing competency based training programs.* Englewood Cliffs, NJ: Prentice-Hall.

Davies, I.K. (1981). *Instructional technique.* New York: McGraw-Hill.

Dick, W., & Carey, L. (1985). *The systematic design of instruction.* Glenview, IL: Scott, Foresman.

Gropper, G. (1991). *Text displays analysis and systematic design.* Englewood Cliffs, NJ: Educational Technology Publications.

Mager, R. (1988). *Making instruction work.* Belmont, CA: Lake Publishing Company.

Mager, R. (1984). *Preparing instructional objectives* (2nd ed., rev.). Belmont, CA: Lake Publishing Company.

McArdle, G.E.H. (1991). *Developing instructional design: A step by step guide to success.* Los Altos, CA: Crisp Publications.

McLagan, P., & O'Brien, M. (1992). *Designshop: Customer-focused instructional design.* St. Paul, MN: McLagan International.

Misanchuk, E. (1992). *Preparing instructional text: Document design using desktop publishing.* Englewood Cliffs, NJ: Educational Technology Publications.

Nilson, C. (1989). *Training program workbook and kit.* Englewood Cliffs, NJ: Prentice-Hall.

Rossett, A., & Gautier-Downes, J. (1991). *A handbook of job aids.* San Diego, CA: Pfeiffer & Company.

Rothwell, W.J., & Kazanas, H.C. (1992). *Mastering the instructional design process: A systematic approach.* San Francisco: Jossey-Bass.

Sibbet, D. (1991). *Fundamentals of graphic images.* Rockbridge Baths, VA: Graphic Guides.

Smith, B.J., & Delahaye, B.L. (1983). *How to be an effective trainer: Skills for managers and new trainers* (2nd ed.). New York: John Wiley & Sons.

Stimson, N. (1991). *How to write and prepare training materials*. London, England: Kogan Page.

Stoneall, L. (1991). *How to write training materials*. San Diego, CA: Pfeiffer & Company.

Editing: **Carol Nolde**
Production Editing: **Dawn Kilgore**
Cover Design, Interior Design, and Illustrations: **Lee Ann Hubbard**

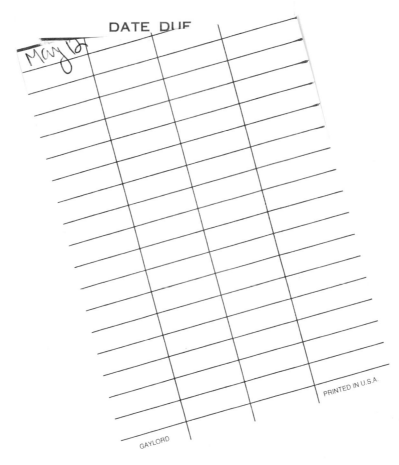

DATE DUE

May 6

GAYLORD

PRINTED IN U.S.A.